Prolegomena

Immanuel Kant

PROLEGOMENA

To Any Future Metaphysics That Will Be Able To Come Forward As Science

The Paul Carus Translation
extensively revised by
James W. Ellington

HACKETT PUBLISHING COMPANY
Indianapolis/Cambridge

Immanuel Kant: 1724–1804

Library of Congress Cataloging in Publication Data

Kant, Immanuel, 1724-1804.
Kant's Prolegomena to any future metaphysics that will be able to come.

Bibliography: p.
1. Metaphysics. 2. Knowledge, Theory of. I. Carus,
Paul, 1852-1919. II. Ellington, James Wesley
III. Title: IV. Title: Prolegomena to any future
metaphysics that will be able to come forward as science.
B2787.E5C3   1976   110   76-51051
ISBN 0-915144-33-6
ISBN 0-915144-25-5 (pbk.)

The paper used in this publication meets the minimum requirements of American National Standard for Information Sciences—Permanence of Paper for Printed Library Materials, ANSI Z39.48-1984.
♾

CONTENTS

FOREWORD

The present translation of Kant's *Prolegomena* is a rather extensive revision of the Paul Carus rendition (Chicago, 1902). Carus made extensive use of John P. Mahaffy's English version of the *Prolegomena* (London, 1872), and Mahaffy made use of John Richardson's rendering (London, 1819). Each successive revision was an improvement over its predecessor, and I can make the same claim for my version without offending anyone by a display of excessive pride. After all, by the fourth round any reader can reasonably expect an accurate and faithful rendering of Kant's original.

I have made use of Karl Vorländer's German text (Leipzig, 1905) as it appears in Vol. III of the Philosophische Bibliothek edition of Kant's works and Benno Erdmann's text (Berlin, 1911) as it appears in Vol. IV of the Königliche Preussische Akademie der Wissenschaften edition of Kant's works. Page numbers of the latter edition, the standard reference for Kant's works, appear in the present translation as marginal numbers. All material interpolated by me in text or notes has been bracketed.

University of Connecticut,   James W. Ellington
Storrs
October 1976

INTRODUCTION

Kant's philosophical excogitations culminated in three grand books entitled *Critique of Pure Reason, Critique of Practical Reason,* and *Critique of Judgment.* The areas covered by these books correspond roughly to those areas designated by Aristotle as the theoretical, practical (moral and political), and productive (aesthetic). All three books are quite technical and difficult; but none of them "fell deadborn from the press," as Hume said had been the fate of his grand book entitled *A Treatise of Human Nature.* To remedy this unfortunate state of affairs, Hume popularized the doctrines of his *Treatise* in two other books entitled *An Inquiry Concerning Human Understanding* and *An Inquiry Concerning the Principles of Morals.* Kant did not exactly popularize his first two *Critiques* when he composed two shorter works entitled *Prolegomena to Any Future Metaphysics* and *Grounding for the Metaphysics of Morals,* but these books do serve as introductions of sorts to the first two critiques and are very likely the most widely read of all Kant's works.

Toward the end of the Preface of the *Prolegomena,* Kant cautions that this work is properly a sequel to the *Critique of Pure Reason,* inasmuch as the former affords the reader a compact overall view of the latter and is written in a manner that makes the doctrines of the *Critique* more accessible than they are in the *Critique* itself. This is to say that in case a reading of the *Critique* has given one largely a view of the trees, a reading of the *Prolegomena* may help give one a view of the forest. In spite of Kant's warning, much can be learned about the Kantian epistemology and metaphysics from a careful reading of the *Prolegomena* before one plunges into the intricacies of the *Critique* or even if one never takes that plunge at all.

The *Prolegomena* is based on an analytical method of exposition which proceeds regressively from conditioned to condition, whereas the *Critique* is based on a synthetical method that proceeds progressively from condition to conditioned. In the *Prolegomena* one starts with some uncontested pure knowledge (e.g., arithmetic and geometry) and needs not inquire as to *whether* such knowledge is possible, since it is already actual, but needs to inquire only as to *how* such knowledge is possible (because time and space are given as pure intuitions). In other words, the apriority of time and space is established merely by the fact that arithmetic and geometry do already exist as pure nonempirical sciences. The synthetical examination of the apriority of time and space in the *Critique* is considerably more intricate; the same is true of the synthetical examination of all the other doctrines of the *Critique* (a priori basis of the necessary connection between cause and effect, the fact that the sensible intuitions of phenomena are extensive magnitudes, and so on). Because of this analytical treatment, the *Prolegomena* readily provides one with the broad outlines of the Kantian system of epistemology and metaphysics.

Kant holds that consciousness (the transcendental unity of apperception) is the very beginning of all speculative philosophy, much as Descartes held the *cogito* in his *Meditations* and also in the *Principles of Philosophy,* Part I, Principle VII, when he asserts that the *I think, therefore I am* is the first and most certain knowledge which can occur to one who philosophizes in an orderly fashion. But Kant differs from Descartes in that he holds that we do not know our noumenal selves by any act of rational intuition (light of nature). For Kant, pure apperception is an act of spontaneity and as such is different from sensibility, which is a passive receptivity for sensible intuitions. The self for Kant becomes aware of itself and gains knowledge of itself only by bringing to self-consciousness (through a transcendental act of synthesis) the manifold of intuitions provided by sensibility. Accordingly, the self knows itself only as an appearance (phenomenon).

In the "Sixth Meditation" Descartes tries to show that the existence of material objects is dependent on an inference from immediate inner experience. But Kant claims (in the *Critique* at B 274-279) that inner experience is not possible unless we have immediate consciousness of external things. External experience of objects is for Kant immediate and not mediate. Inner experience is not immediate (as Descartes claimed) but is possible only mediately through the experience of actual things. Our perception of external objects is possible only by means of time and space, which are the forms of all sensible intuition. Kant's views on time and space developed largely as an opposition to the positions of Leibniz and Newton. Leibniz had claimed that the universe is composed of monads, which are simple, immaterial (spiritual) substances. Each monad has some degree of consciousness. Space was thought of as being a set of relations that monads have to each other; it is the order of coexistent things. Time was thought of as being the relations of the successive states of consciousness of a single monad. Accordingly, for Leibniz space and time were relations among things (monads) and would have no existence whatever if there were no monads. By contrast, Newton held that space and time are infinite and independent of the physical bodies that exist in space and time. For him, space and time were things and would exist even if there were no bodies. He held that there are absolute positions in space and time which are independent of the material entities occupying them and, furthermore, that empty space (void) and empty time are possible. Leibniz denied both tenets.

For Kant, space and time are based epistemologically on the nature of the mind rather than ontologically on the nature of things, either as a relation among monads (Leibniz) or as things (Newtonian absolute space and absolute time). Kant's epistemological view of space and time provided him with a way of reconciling the opposed views of Leibniz and Newton. Space and time are indeed the relational orders of contemporaneous objects and successive states, inasmuch as space and time are the conditions of intuitive representations of objects rather than being mere relations of independent substances (monads). Space and time are indeed absolute wholes in which physical objects are located, inasmuch as they are forms of sensible intuition lying ready in the mind rather than being independently existing containers for physical objects.

Geometry is based on the pure intuition of space. When one says that a straight line is the shortest distance between two points, he makes an appeal to spatial intuition. The concept of straight is merely qualitative. The concept of shortest is not already contained in the concept of straight but is an addition to straight through recourse to the pure intuition of space. Accordingly, the propositions of geometry are not analytic but a priori synthetic. So are the propositions of arithmetic. The concept of number is achieved by the successive addition of units in the pure intuition of time. Leibniz had claimed that the propositions of mathematics are analytic.

When one turns from mathematics to the realm of natural science and encounters physical entities, he finds that Kant espoused a form of realism which he calls transcendental idealism. In this view one has a problematic concept of the thing-in-itself lying at the basis of a real object and a determinate concept of the object as an appearance. This position is very close to that of Locke when he claims that we do not have an adequate knowledge of the real essence of substances but we do have an adequate knowledge of the nominal essence of them. Kant repudiated the idealism of Berkeley and the phenomenalism of Hume when they claimed that a physical object is nothing but a cluster of qualities existing in some mind. For Kant there is a reality behind the appearance, but one has only a problematic concept of that reality. One has an actual and detailed knowledge of appearances; but appearances are not all that there is, as Berkeley and Hume claimed.

Nature for Kant is the existence of such real objects as they are ordered according to universal laws. The laws that order nature in general are a priori, whereas the laws that order nature in particular (chemical phenomena, hydrostatic, botanical, bovine, and so forth) are a posteriori. These most general laws of nature include those that tell us the following: the intuitions of phenomena are extensive magnitudes, substance is the permanent substratum underlying all change, all changes of phenomena take place in conformity with the law of the connection of cause and effect, substances stand in a relation of reciprocal causality regarding their accidents, etc. In maintaining the apriority of such universal laws of nature, Kant obviously places himself squarely in the continental rationalistic tradition of Descartes and Leibniz rather than in the tradition of the British empiricists. This becomes quite clear when one compares Hume's treatment of the idea of the necessary connection between cause and effect with Kant's treatment.

The locus classicus of the Kantian treatment of efficient causation is to be found in the Second Analogy of Experience in the "Transcendental Analytic" of the *Critique of Pure Reason* (and in §'s 27, 28, 29 of the *Prolegomena*), where a subjective connection of cognitions is distinguished from an objective connection of them. One walks into a warm room and a little later sees a glowing stove. As far as the subjective order of cognitions is concerned, one first feels warm and only later spots the stove concealed behind a screen in the corner. But yet one says that the stove causes the room to be warm and not that the warm room causes the stove to glow. In order to have knowledge through perception, one must connect his sense perceptions in their objective time relations. There is no necessity in the subjective order of cognitions, but there certainly is in one's synthetic reorganization of that order. If event A (glowing stove) precedes event B (warm room) objectively, then one must think of A as preceding B or else be wrong. It makes no difference whether one perceives A first and then B, or B first and then A in his subjective consciousness.

Hume had claimed that there are three conditions that two events must fulfill in order for one event to be considered the cause of another. The cause precedes the effect in time, cause and effect are contiguous in space, and cause and effect are found constantly conjoined in experience. Kant leveled his attack mainly against the third condition, but other people have found objections to the first two conditions as well. In the realm of colliding billiard balls, the cause does precede the effect in time. But in the case of boiling water, the boiling takes place just when the water reaches 100°C.; and so cause and effect are simultaneous. As for spatial contiguity, the moon through empty space attracts the waters of the earth's seas and oceans to produce tides. In the case of such action at a distance, there is no contiguity in space. As for constant conjunction, some have pointed out that night and day are always conjoined, but night is not the cause of day.

Kant objected to the third condition by claiming that on Hume's view there is no way to distinguish the subjective order of cognitions from the objective. In the Preface to the *Prolegomena* Kant says that it was Hume's treatment of causation that first interrupted his dogmatic slumber in the German traditional Leibniz–Wolff–Baumgarten philosophy and started him on his own critical line of thought. Hume held that the idea of necessary connection between cause and effect arises when we develop a habit of association from a repeated subjective succession of perceptions (fire always burns). He thus based causation entirely on sensible experience. In contrast, Kant claimed that the objective reordering of the subjective succession of cognitions (which is based on sense perception and imagination) is actually a synthetic reorganization of the a posteriori order of perception. This synthetic reorganization is an a priori act of the human understanding. In other words, the causal ordering of cognitions is an act of the intellect that is *brought to* experience (or, better still, that *makes* experience) and is not an ordering derived *from* experience (as Hume claimed). For Kant, pure concepts such as those of substance, cause, possibility, existence, and necessity are coterminous with the pure forms of intuition, time and space. Experience is the result of the synthetic activity of the intellect by means of such pure concepts in organizing empirically given sense perceptions which are arrayed in time and space.

When such a priori concepts (e.g., substance and existence) are employed so as to try to determine something about supersensible objects rather than mere sensible objects, such employment oversteps the bounds of all possible experience and produces illusion. Like the rationalists, Kant claims that there are a priori forms of thought; but unlike many of them, he argues that such pure thoughts are meaningful only when they are applied to sense perceptions to organize these perceptions into objective experience. When the concept of substance is applied to the soul in order to infer its permanence (immortality), the concept is employed transcendently, and there results not objective knowledge but dialectical illusion. Such employment is illegitimate for Kant, and hence such pure use of reason must be criticized. Kant and Hume have much in common in their criticism of the attempts of reason to transcend all possible sense experience.

Nowhere does this similarity show up so clearly as in their criticism of the ontological proof for the existence of God. Early in

Part IX of the *Dialogues Concerning Natural Religion* Hume has Demea say: "We must, therefore, have recourse to a necessarily existent Being, who carries the REASON of his existence in himself; and who cannot be supposed not to exist without an express contradiction. There is consequently such a Being, that is, there is a Deity." Philo refutes the argument by saying that any matter of fact (synthetic truth) cannot be proved by any a priori arguments (deductive proofs such as one finds in mathematics and logic). Whatever can be conceived as existent can also be conceived as nonexistent (e.g., the sun may not rise tomorrow). There is no Being whose nonexistence implies a contradiction. Hence there are no analytic proofs for establishing the existence of God. To establish such existence one would have to turn to the evidence of the senses, but in the case of a Supreme Being the senses are dumb.

In the Ideal of Pure Reason to be found in the "Transcendental Dialectic" of the *Critique of Pure Reason* (B 595-670), Kant claims that there are only three possible proofs for the existence of God: the physico-theological, the cosmological, and the ontological. The first two depend on the third; if the third falls, so do the first two. At B 626 (in the N. K. Smith translation) he asserts: "But if . . . we admit, as every reasonable person must, that all existential propositions are synthetic, how can we profess to maintain that the predicate of existence cannot be rejected without contradiction? This is a feature which is found only in analytic propositions, and is indeed what constitutes their analytic character." And at B 630 he maintains that "since the criterion of the possibility of synthetic knowledge is never to be looked for save in experience, to which the object of an idea [e.g., God] cannot belong, the connection of all real properties in a thing is a synthesis, the possibility of which we are unable to determine a priori [but can determine only a posteriori]."

This introduction is intended to provide the reader with a brief survey of some of the most outstanding mountain peaks dotting the landscape of the Kantian system of epistemology and metaphysics. For a fuller view of these peaks, as well as a view of still other peaks and of all the valleys comprising that landscape, the reader must now turn to the *Prolegomena* and perhaps later (as is highly desirable) to the *Critique of Pure Reason* itself.

SELECTED BIBLIOGRAPHY

PROLEGOMENA

Apel, Max, *Kommentar zu Kants Prolegomena. Eine Einführung in die kritische Philosophie.* Second revised edition. (Leipzig, 1923).

Erdmann, Benno, *Historische Studien über Kants Prolegomena.* (Halle, 1904).

(There are few works in English specifically devoted to a study of the *Prolegomena.* However, one often finds references to the *Prolegomena* in studies devoted to the *Critique of Pure Reason.*)

GENERAL WORKS ON KANT'S EPISTEMOLOGY AND METAPHYSICS

Beck, L. W., *Early German Philosophy: Kant and his Predecessors.* (Harvard, 1969). Chapter XVII.

Gram, Moltke, *Kant, Ontology, and the A Priori.* (Northwestern, 1968).

Melnick, Arthur, *Kant's Analogies of Experience.* (Chicago, 1973).

Paton, H. J., *Kant's Metaphysic of Experience: A Commentary on the First Half of the Kritik der reinen Vernunft,* 2 vols. (London, 1936).

de Vleeschauwer, Herman-J., *The Development of Kantian Thought* (trans. A.R.C. Duncan). (London, 1962).

Weldon, T. D., *Introduction to Kant's Critique of Pure Reason.* (Oxford, 1945).

Wolff, Robert P., *Kant's Theory of Mental Activity.* (Harvard, 1963).

Prolegomena

zu

einer jeden

künftigen Metaphysik

die

als Wissenschaft

wird auftreten können,

von

Immanuel Kant.

Riga,

bey Johann Friedrich Hartknoch.

1783.

PREFACE

These *Prolegomena* are not for the use of pupils but of future   255
teachers, and even the latter should not expect that they will be
serviceable for the systematic exposition of a ready-made
science, but merely for the discovery of the science itself.
There are scholars for whom the history of philosophy (both
ancient and modern) is philosophy itself; for these the present
Prolegomena are not written. They must wait till those who
endeavor to draw from the fountain of reason itself have completed their work; it will then be the turn of such scholars to
inform the world of what has been done. Unfortunately, nothing
can be said which, in their opinion, has not been said before, and
truly the same prophecy applies to all future time; for since the
human reason has for many centuries speculated upon innumer-
able objects in various ways, it is hardly to be expected that we
should not be able to discover analogies for every new idea
among the old sayings of past ages.

My object is to persuade all those who think metaphysics
worth studying that it is absolutely necessary to pause a moment
and, disregarding all that has been done, to propose first the preliminary question, "Whether such a thing as metaphysics be at
all possible?"

If it is a science, how does it happen that it cannot, like other
sciences, obtain universal and permanent recognition? If not,
how can it maintain its pretensions and keep the human under-   256
standing in suspense with hopes never ceasing, yet never
fulfilled? Whether then we demonstrate our knowledge or our
ignorance in this field, we must come once for all to a definite
conclusion respecting the nature of this so-called science, which
cannot possibly remain on its present footing. It seems almost
ridiculous, while every other science is continually advancing,

1

that in this, which pretends to be wisdom incarnate, for whose oracle every one inquires, we should constantly move round the same spot, without gaining a single step. And so its supporters having melted away, we do not find that men who are confident of their ability to shine in other sciences venture their reputation here, where everybody, however ignorant in other matters, presumes to deliver a final verdict, inasmuch as in this domain there is as yet no standard weight and measure to distinguish soundness from shallow talk.

After all, it is nothing extraordinary in the elaboration of a science, when men begin to wonder how far it has advanced, that the question should at last occur as to whether and how in general such a science is possible? Human reason so delights in constructions that it has several times built up a tower and then razed it to examine the nature of the foundation. It is never too late to become reasonable and wise; but if the insight comes late, there is always more difficulty in starting the change.

The question whether a science be possible presupposes a doubt as to its actuality. But such a doubt offends the man whose entire goods may perhaps consist in this supposed jewel; hence he who raises the doubt must expect opposition from all sides. Some, in the proud consciousness of their possessions, which are ancient and therefore considered legitimate, will take their metaphysical compendia in their hands and look down on him with contempt; others who never see anything except it be identical with what they have somewhere else seen before will not understand him, and everything will remain for a time as if nothing had happened to excite the concern or the hope for an impending change.

Nevertheless, I venture to predict that the independent reader of these *Prolegomena* will not only doubt his previous science, but ultimately be fully persuaded that it cannot exist unless the demands here stated on which its possibility depends be satisfied; and, as this has never been done, that there is, as yet, no such thing as metaphysics. But as it can never cease to be in demand[1]—since the interests of human reason in general are

257

1. Says Horace:

   Rusticus expectat, dum defluat amnis, at ille labitur et labetur intimately interwoven with it—he must confess that a radical reform, or rather a rebirth of the science according to a new plan, is unavoidable, however much men may struggle against it for a while.

Since the *Essays* of Locke and Leibniz, or rather since the origin of metaphysics so far as we know its history, nothing has ever happened which could have been more decisive to its fate than the attack made upon it by David Hume. He threw no light on this kind of knowledge; but he certainly struck a spark from which light might have been obtained, had it caught some inflammable substance and had its smouldering fire been carefully nursed and developed.

Hume started mainly from a single but important concept in metaphysics, namely, that of the connection of cause and effect (including its derivative concepts of force and action, etc.). He challenged reason, which pretends to have given birth to this concept of herself, to answer him by what right she thinks anything could be so constituted that if that thing be posited, something else also must necessarily be posited; for this is the meaning of the concept of cause. He demonstrated irrefutably that it was entirely impossible for reason to think *a priori* and by means of concepts such a combination as involves necessity. We cannot at all see why, in consequence of the existence of one thing, another must necessarily exist, or how the concept of such a combination can arise *a priori*. Hence he inferred that reason was altogether deluded with reference to this concept, which she erroneously considered as one of her children, whereas in reality it was nothing but a bastard of imagination, impregnated by ex- 258 perience, which subsumed certain representations under the law of association, and mistook a subjective necessity (custom) for an objective necessity arising from insight. Hence he inferred that reason had no power to think such connections, even in general, because her concepts would then be purely fictitious and all her pretended *a priori* cognitions nothing but common experiences marked with a false stamp. This is as much as to say

---

in omne volubilis aevum. ["A peasant waits for the river to flow away, but it flows on and will so flow forever."] *Epistle* I, 2, 42f.

that there is not, and cannot be, any such thing as metaphysics at all.[2]

However hasty and mistaken Hume's conclusion may appear, it was at least founded upon investigation, and this investigation deserved the concentrated attention of the brighter spirits of his day as well as determined efforts on their part to discover, if possible, a happier solution of the problem in the sense proposed by him, all of which would have speedily resulted in a complete reform of the science.

But Hume suffered the usual misfortune of metaphysicians, of not being understood. It is positively painful to see how utterly his opponents, Reid, Oswald, Beattie, and lastly Priestley, missed the point of the problem; for while they were ever taking for granted that which he doubted, and demonstrating with zeal and often with impudence that which he never thought of doubting, they so misconstrued his valuable suggestion that everything remained in its old condition, as if nothing had happened. The question was not whether the concept of cause was right, useful, and even indispensable for our knowledge of nature, for this Hume had never doubted; but whether that concept could be thought by reason *a priori*, and consequently whether it possessed an inner truth, independent of all experience, implying a more widely extended usefulness, not limited merely to objects of experience. This was Hume's problem. It was a question concerning the *origin* of the concept, not concerning its indispensability in use. Were the former decided, the conditions of its use and the sphere of its valid application would have been determined as a matter of course.

But to satisfy the conditions of the problem, the opponents of the great thinker should have penetrated very deeply into the

259

2. Nevertheless Hume called such destructive philosophy metaphysics and attached to it great value. "Metaphysics and morals," he says, "are the most important branches of science; mathematics and natural philosophy are not half so important." [*Essays Moral, Politcal, and Literary* (edited by Green and Grose) vol. I, p. 187. Essay XIV: Of the Rise and Progress of the Arts and Sciences] But the acute man merely regarded the negative use arising from the moderation of extravagant claims of speculative reason, and the complete settlement of the many endless and troublesome controversies that mislead mankind. He overlooked the positive injury which results if reason be deprived of its most important prospects, which can alone supply to the will the highest aim for all its endeavors.

nature of reason, so far as it is concerned with pure thought—a task which did not suit them. They found a more convenient method of being defiant without any insight, viz., the appeal to *common sense.* It is indeed a great gift of heaven to possess right or (as they now call it) plain common sense. But this common sense must be shown in deeds by well-considered and reasonable thoughts and words, not by appealing to it as an oracle when no rational justification of oneself can be advanced. To appeal to common sense when insight and science fail, and no sooner— this is one of the subtle discoveries of modern times, by means of which the most superficial ranter can safely enter the lists with the most thorough thinker and hold his own. But as long as a particle of insight remains, no one would think of having recourse to this subterfuge. Seen in a clear light, it is but an appeal to the opinion of the multitude, of whose applause the philosopher is ashamed, while the popular charlatan glories and confides in it. I should think that Hume might fairly have laid as much claim to common sense as Beattie and, in addition, to a critical reason (such as the latter did not possess), which keeps common sense in check and prevents it from speculating, or, if speculations are under discussion, restrains the desire to decide because it cannot satisfy itself concerning its own principles. By this means alone can common sense remain sound. Chisels and hammers may suffice to work a piece of wood, but for etching we require an etcher's needle. Thus common sense and speculative understanding are both useful, but each in its own 260 way: the former in judgments which apply immediately to experience; the latter when we judge universally from mere concepts, as in metaphysics, where sound common sense, so called in spite of the inappropriateness of the word, has no right to judge at all.

I openly confess that my remembering David Hume was the very thing which many years ago first interrupted my dogmatic slumber and gave my investigations in the field of speculative philosophy a quite new direction. I was far from following him in the conclusions to which he arrived by considering, not the whole of his problem, but a part, which by itself can give us no information. If we start from a well-founded, but undeveloped, thought which another has bequeathed to us, we may well hope by continued reflection to advance further than the acute man to whom we owe the first spark of light.

So I tried first whether Hume's objection could not be put into a general form, and soon found that the concept of the connection of cause and effect was by no means the only concept by which the understanding thinks the connection of things *a priori,* but rather that metaphysics consists altogether of such concepts. I sought to ascertain their number; and when I had satisfactorily succeeded in this by starting from a single principle, I proceeded to the deduction of these concepts, which I was now certain were not derived from experience, as Hume had tried, but sprang from the pure understanding. This deduction (which seemed impossible to my acute predecessor and had never even occurred to any one else, though no one had hesitated to use the concepts without investigating the basis of their objective validity) was the most difficult task ever undertaken in the service of metaphysics; and the worst was that metaphysics, such as it then existed, could not assist me in the least because this deduction alone can render metaphysics possible. But as soon as I had succeeded in solving Hume's problem, not merely in a particular 261 case, but with respect to the whole faculty of pure reason, I could proceed safely, though slowly, to determine the whole sphere of pure reason completely and from universal principles, in its boundaries as well as in its contents. This was required for metaphysics in order to construct its system according to a sure plan.

But I fear that the working out of Hume's problem in its widest extent (namely, my *Critique of Pure Reason*) will fare as the problem itself fared when first proposed. It will be misjudged because it is misunderstood, and misunderstood because men choose to skim through the book and not to think through it—a disagreeable task, because the work is dry, obscure, opposed to all ordinary notions, and moreover long-winded. Now I confess that I did not expect to hear from philosophers complaints of want of popularity, entertainment, and facility when the existence of a highly prized and indispensable cognition is at stake, which cannot be established otherwise than by the strictest rules of scholarly precision. Popularity may follow, but is inadmissible at the beginning. Yet as regards a certain obscurity, arising partly from the diffuseness of the plan, owing to which the principal points of the investigation are easily lost sight of, the complaint is just, and I intend to remove it by the present *Prolegomena.*

The first-mentioned work, which discusses the pure faculty of reason in its whole extent and bounds, will remain the foundation, to which the *Prolegomena,* as a preliminary exercise, refer; for that critique must exist as a science, systematic and complete as to its smallest parts, before we can think of letting metaphysics appear on the scene, or even have the most distant hope of so doing.

We have been long accustomed to seeing antiquated knowledge produced as new by taking it out of its former context, and fitting it into a systematic dress of any fancy pattern under new titles. Most readers will set out by expecting nothing else from the *Critique;* but these *Prolegomena* may persuade him that it is a perfectly new science, of which no one has ever even thought, **262** the very idea of which was unknown, and for which nothing hitherto accomplished can be of the smallest use, except it be the suggestion of Hume's doubts. Yet even he did not suspect such a formal science, but ran his ship ashore, for safety's sake, landing on scepticism, there to let it lie and rot; whereas my object is rather to give it a pilot who, by means of safe navigational principles drawn from a knowledge of the globe and provided with a complete chart and compass, may steer the ship safely whither he listeth.

If in a new science that is wholly isolated and unique in its kind we started with the prejudice that we can judge of things by means of would-be knowledge previously acquired, even though this is precisely what has first to be called in question; then we should only fancy we saw everywhere what we had already known, because the expressions have a similar sound. Yet everything would appear utterly metamorphosed, senseless, and unintelligible, because we should have as a foundation our own thoughts, made by long habit a second nature, instead of the author's. However, the longwindedness of the work, so far as it depends on the science itself and not on the exposition, its consequent unavoidable dryness, and its scholastic precision are qualities which can only benefit the science, though they may discredit the book.

Few writers are gifted with the subtlety and, at the same time, with the grace of David Hume, or with the depth, as well as the elegance, of Moses Mendelssohn. Yet I flatter myself that I might have made my own exposition popular, if my object had been merely to sketch out a plan and leave its completion to others, instead of having my heart in the welfare of the science to which I had devoted myself so long; in truth, it required no little constancy, and even self-denial, to postpone the sweets of an immediate success to the prospect of a slower, but more lasting, reputation.

Making plans is often the occupation of an opulent and boastful mind, which thus obtains the reputation of a creative genius by demanding what it cannot itself supply, by censuring what it cannot improve, and by proposing what it knows not where to find. And yet something more should belong to a sound plan of a general critique of pure reason than mere conjectures, if this plan is to be other than the usual declamations of pious aspirations. But pure reason is a sphere so separate and self-contained that we cannot touch a part without affecting all the rest. We can therefore do nothing without first determining the position of each part and its relation to the rest. For inasmuch as our judgment cannot be corrected by anything outside of pure reason, so the validity and use of every part depends upon the relation in which it stands to all the rest within the domain of reason, just as in the structure of an organized body the end of each member can only be deduced from the full conception of the whole. It may, then, be said of such a critique that it is never trustworthy except it be perfectly complete, down to the smallest elements of pure reason. In the sphere of this faculty you can determine either everything or nothing.

But although a mere sketch preceding the *Critique of Pure Reason* would be unintelligible, unreliable, and useless, it is all the more useful as a sequel which enables us to grasp the whole, to examine in detail the chief points of importance in the science, and to improve in many respects our exposition, as compared with the first execution of the work.

That work being completed, I offer here such a plan which is sketched out after an analytical method, while the *Critique* itself had to be executed in the synthetical style, in order that the science may present all its articulations, as the structure of a peculiar cognitive faculty, in their natural combination. But should any reader find this plan, which I publish as the *Prolegomena to Any Future Metaphysics,* still obscure, let him consider that not every one is bound to study metaphysics, that

263

many minds will succeed very well in the exact and even in deep sciences more closely allied to intuition while they cannot succeed in investigations dealing exclusively with abstract concepts. In such cases men should apply their talents to other subjects. **264** But he who undertakes to judge or, still more, to construct a system of metaphysics must satisfy the demands here made, either by adopting my solution or by thoroughly refuting it and substituting another. To evade it is impossible. In conclusion, let it be remembered that this much-abused obscurity (frequently serving as a mere pretext under which people hide their own indolence or dullness) has its uses, since all who in other sciences observe a judicious silence speak authoritatively in metaphysics and make bold decisions, because their ignorance is not here contrasted with the knowledge of others. Yet it does contrast with sound critical principles, which we may therefore commend in the words of Virgil:

Ignavum, fucos, pecus a praesepibus arcent.[3]

3. ["They keep out of the hives the drones, an indolent bunch."] *Georgics,* IV 168.

*Preamble on the Peculiarities of all
Metaphysical Cognition*

§1. OF THE SOURCES OF METAPHYSICS

If it becomes desirable to present any cognition as science, it will be necessary first to determine exactly its differentia, which no other science has in common with it and which constitutes its peculiarity; otherwise the boundaries of all sciences become confused, and none of them can be treated thoroughly according to its nature.

The peculiar features of a science may consist of a simple difference of object, or of the sources of cognition, or of the kind of cognition, or perhaps of all three conjointly. On these features, therefore, depends the idea of a possible science and its territory.

First, as concerns the sources of metaphysical cognition, its very concept implies that they cannot be empirical. Its principles (including not only its basic propositions but also its basic concepts) must never be derived from experience. It must not be physical but metaphysical knowledge, i.e., knowledge lying beyond experience. It can therefore have for its basis neither external experience, which is the source of physics proper, nor internal, which is the basis of empirical psychology. It is therefore *a priori* cognition, coming from pure understanding and 266 pure reason.

But so far metaphysics would not be distinguishable from pure mathematics; it must therefore be called pure philosophical cognition; and for the meaning of this term I refer to the *Critique of Pure Reason* ("Methodology", Chap. I, Sec. 1), where the distinction between these two employments of reason is sufficiently explained. So much for the sources of metaphysical cognition.

§ 2. CONCERNING THE KIND OF COGNITION
WHICH CAN ALONE BE CALLED METAPHYSICAL

a. Of the Distinction between Analytic and Synthetic Judgments in General.—The peculiarity of its sources demands that metaphysical cognition must consist of nothing but *a priori* judgments. But whatever be their origin or their logical form, there is a distinction in judgments, as to their content, according to which they are either merely *explicative*, adding nothing to the content of the cognition, or *ampliative*, increasing the given cognition: the former may be called *analytic*, the latter *synthetic*, judgments.

Analytic judgments express nothing in the predicate but what has been already actually thought in the concept of the subject, though not so clearly and with the same consciousness. If I say: "All bodies are extended," I have not amplified in the least my concept of body, but have only analyzed it, as extension was really thought to belong to that concept before the judgment was made, though it was not expressed; this judgment is therefore analytic. On the other hand, this judgment, "Some bodies have weight," contains in its predicate something not actually thought in the universal concept of body; it amplifies my knowledge by adding something to my concept, and must therefore be called synthetic.

b. The Common Principle of all Analytic Judgments is that of Contradiction.—All analytic judgments depend wholly on the principle of contradiction, and are in their nature *a priori* cognitions, whether the concepts that supply them with matter be empirical or not. For the predicate of an affirmative analytic judgment is already thought in the concept of the subject, of which it cannot be denied without contradiction. In the same way its opposite is necessarily denied of the subject in an analytic, but negative, judgment, by the same principle of contradiction. Such is the case of the judgments: "All bodies are extended," and "No bodies are unextended (i.e., simple)."

For this very reason all analytic judgments are *a priori* even when the concepts are empirical, as, for example, "Gold is a yellow metal"; for to know this I require no experience beyond my concept of gold, which contained the thought that this body is yellow and metal. It is, in fact, this thought that constituted my

267

concept; and I need only analyze it, without looking beyond it elsewhere.

c. Synthetic Judgments Require a Different Principle from that of Contradiction.—There are synthetic *a posteriori* judgments of empirical origin; but there are also others which are certain *a priori*, and which spring from pure understanding and reason. Yet they both agree in this, that they cannot possibly spring from the principle of analysis, namely, the principle of contradiction, alone, but require another quite different principle. But whatever principle they may be deduced from, they must be subject to the principle of contradiction, which must never be violated, even though everything cannot be deduced from it. I shall first classify synthetic judgments.

1. *Judgments of Experience* are always synthetic. For it would be absurd to base an analytic judgment on experience, as our concept suffices for the purpose without requiring any testimony from experience. That a body is extended is a judgment which holds *a priori*, and is not a judgment of experience. For before appealing to experience, we already have all the conditions for the judgment in the concept, from which we have then but to elicit the predicate according to the principle of contradiction, and thereby to become conscious of the necessity of the judgment, which experience could not at all teach us.

2. *Mathematical Judgments* are all synthetic. This fact seems hitherto to have altogether escaped the observation of those who have analyzed human reason; it even seems directly opposed to all their conjectures, though it is incontestably certain and most important in its consequences. For as it was found that the conclusions of mathematicians all proceed according to the principle of contradiction (as is demanded by all apodeictic certainty), men persuaded themselves that the fundamental propositions were known from the principle of contradiction. This was a great mistake, for a synthetic proposition can indeed be comprehended according to the principle of contradiction, but only by presupposing another synthetic proposition from which it follows, but never in and by itself.

First of all, we must observe that properly mathematical propositions are always judgments *a priori*, and not empirical, because they carry with them necessity, which cannot be obtained

268

from experience. But if this be not conceded to me, very well; I shall confine my assertion to *pure mathematics,* the very concept of which implies that it contains pure *a priori* and not empirical cognition.

It might at first be thought that the proposition 7 + 5 = 12 is a mere analytic judgment, following from the concept of the sum of seven and five, according to the principle of contradiction. But on closer examination it appears that the concept of the sum of 7 + 5 contains merely their union in a single number, without its being at all thought what the particular number is that unites them. The concept of twelve is by no means thought by merely thinking of the combination of seven and five; and, analyze this possible sum as we may, we shall not discover twelve in the concept. We must go beyond these concepts by calling to our aid some intuition corresponding to one of them, i.e., either our five fingers or five points (as Segner[4] has it in his *Arithmetic*); and we must add successively the units of the five given in the intuition to the concept of seven. Hence our concept is really amplified by the proposition 7 + 5 = 12, and we add to the first concept a second one not thought in it. Arithmetical judgments are therefore synthetic, and the more plainly according as we take larger numbers; for in such cases it is clear that, however closely we analyze our concepts without calling intuition to our aid, we can never find the sum by such mere analysis.

All principles of pure geometry are no less synthetic. That a straight line is the shortest path between two points is a synthetic proposition. For my concept of straight contains nothing of quantity, but only a quality. The concept of the shortest is therefore altogether additional and cannot be obtained by any analysis of the concept of the straight line. Here, too, intuition must come to aid us. It alone makes the synthesis possible.

(Some other principles, assumed by geometers, are indeed actually analytic and depend on the principle of contradiction; but they only serve, as identical propositions, as a method of concatenation, and not as principles, e.g., *a = a,* the whole is equal to itself, or *a + b> a,* the whole is greater than its part. And yet even these, though they are recognized as valid from mere con-

---

4. [J. A. Segner: *Elementa Arithmeticae et Geometriae,* Göttingen, 1739.]

cepts, are only admitted in mathematics because they can be presented in some intuition.) What actually makes us believe that the predicate of such apodeictic judgments is already contained in our concept, and that the judgment is therefore analytic, is the duplicity of the expression. We must think a certain predicate as joined to a given concept, and this necessity inheres in the concepts themselves. But the question is not what we must join in thought *to* the given concept, but what we actually think together with and in it, though obscurely; and so it is manifest that the predicate belongs to this concept necessarily indeed, yet not directly but indirectly by means of a necessarily present intuition.[5]

The essential and distinguishing feature of pure mathematical 272 cognition among all other *a priori* cognitions is that it cannot at all proceed from concepts, but only by means of the construction of concepts (see *Critique of Pure Reason,* "Methodology", Chap. I, Sect. 1). As therefore in its judgments it must proceed beyond the concept to that which its corresponding intuition contains, these judgments neither can, nor ought to arise analytically, by dissecting the concept, but are all synthetic.

I cannot refrain from pointing out the disadvantage resulting to philosophy from the neglect of this easy and apparently insignificant observation. Hume, feeling the call (which is worthy of a philosopher) to cast his eye over the whole field of *a priori* cognitions in which human understanding claims such mighty possessions, heedlessly severed from it a whole, and indeed its most valuable, province, viz., pure mathematics. For he imagined that its nature, or, so to speak, the constitution of this province, depended on totally different principles, namely, on the principle of contradiction alone, and although he did not divide judgments in this manner formally and universally and did not use the same terminology as I have done here, what he said was equivalent to this: that pure mathematics contains only analytic, but metaphysics synthetic, *a priori* judgments. In this, however, he was greatly mistaken, and the mistake had a decidedly in-

5. [In the next several pages the order of the German text as it appears in the *Philosophische Bibliothek* Edition of Kant's *Works* is followed rather than the *Akademie* Edition.]

jurious effect upon his whole conception. But for this, he would have extended his question concerning the origin of our synthetic judgments far beyond the metaphysical concept of causality and included in it the possibility of mathematics *a priori* also; for this latter he must have assumed to be equally synthetic. And then he could not have based his metaphysical judgments on mere experience without subjecting the axioms of mathematics equally to experience, a thing which he was far too acute to do. The good company into which metaphysics would thus have been brought would have saved it from the danger of a contemptuous ill-treatment; for the thrust intended for it must have reached mathematics, which was not and could not have been Hume's intention. Thus that acute man would have been led into considerations which must needs be similar to those that now occupy us, but which would have gained inestimably from his inimitably elegant style.

[3.] *Metaphysical Judgments,* properly so-called, are all synthetic. We must distinguish judgments belonging to metaphysics from metaphysical judgments properly so-called. Many of the former are analytic, but they only afford the means to metaphysical judgments, which are the whole aim of the science and which are always synthetic. For if there be concepts belonging to metaphysics (as, for example, that of substance), the judgments springing from simple analysis of them also belong to metaphysics, as, for example, substance is that which only exists as subject, etc. By means of several such analytic judgments we seek to arrive at the definition of a concept. But as the analysis of a pure concept of the understanding (such as metaphysics contains) does not proceed in any different manner from the dissection of any other, even empirical, concepts, not belonging to metaphysics (such as, air is an elastic fluid, the elasticity of which is not destroyed by any known degree of cold), it follows that the concept indeed, but not the analytic judgment, is properly metaphysical. This science has something special and peculiar to itself in the production of its *a priori* cognitions, which must therefore be distinguished from the features it has in common with other rational knowledge. Thus the judgment that all the substance in things is permanent is a synthetic and properly metaphysical judgment.

If the *a priori* concepts which constitute the materials and building blocks of metaphysics have first been collected according to fixed principles, then their analysis will be of great value.

It might be taught as a particular part (as a *philosophia definitiva*), containing nothing but analytic judgments pertaining to metaphysics, and could be treated separately from the synthetic, 274 which constitute metaphysics proper. For indeed these analyses are not elsewhere of much value except in metaphysics, i.e., as regards the synthetic judgments which are to be generated out of these previously analyzed concepts.

The conclusion drawn in this section then is that metaphysics is properly concerned with synthetic propositions *a priori*, and these alone constitute its end, for which it indeed requires various dissections of its concepts, viz., analytic judgments, but wherein the procedure is not different from that in every other kind of cognition, in which we merely seek to render our concepts distinct by analysis. But the generation of *a priori* cognition by intuition as well as by concepts, in fine, of synthetic propositions *a priori* in philosophical cognition, constitutes the essential content of metaphysics.

§ 3. A REMARK ON THE GENERAL DIVISION OF JUDGMENTS   270
INTO ANALYTIC AND SYNTHETIC

This division is indispensable as concerns the critique of human understanding and therefore deserves to be classical in it, though otherwise it is of little use. But this is the reason why dogmatic philosophers, who always seek the sources of metaphysical judgments in metaphysics itself and not outside of it in the pure laws of reason generally, altogether neglected this apparently obvious distinction. Thus the celebrated Wolff and his acute follower Baumgarten came to seek the proof of the principle of sufficient reason, which is clearly synthetic, in the principle of contradiction. In Locke's *Essay,* however, I find an indication of my division. For in the fourth book (chap. iii., § 9, seq.), having discussed the various connections of representations in judgments, and their sources, one of which he makes "identity or contradiction" (analytic judgments) and another the coexistence of representations in a subject (synthetic judgments), he confesses (§10) that our (*a priori*) knowledge of the latter is very narrow and almost nothing. But in his remarks on this species of cognition, there is so little of what is definite and reduced to rules that we cannot wonder if no one, not even Hume, was led to make investigations concerning judgments of this kind. For such universal and yet determinate principles are not easily learned from other men who have only had them obscurely in their minds. One must hit on them first by one's own reflection; then one finds them elsewhere, where one could not possibly have found them at first because the authors themselves did not know that such an idea lay at the basis of their observations. Men who never think independently have nevertheless the acuteness to discover everything, after it has been once shown them, in what was said long since, though no one could ever see it there before.

271   § 4   THE GENERAL QUESTION OF THE PROLEGOMENA:
                      IS METAPHYSICS AT ALL POSSIBLE?

Were a metaphysics, which could maintain its place as a science, really in existence, could we say: here is metaphysics, learn it, and it will convince you irresistibly and irrevocably of its truth? This question would be useless, and there would only remain that other question (which would rather be a test of our acuteness than a proof of the existence of the thing itself): how is the science possible, and how does reason come to attain it? But human reason has not been so fortunate in this case. There is no single book to which you can point, as you do to Euclid, and say: this is metaphysics; here you may find the noblest aim of this science, namely, the knowledge of a highest being, and of a future existence, proved from principles of pure reason. We can be shown indeed many judgments, apodeictically certain, and never questioned; but these are all analytic, and rather concern the materials and the scaffolding for metaphysics than the extension of knowledge, which is our proper object in studying it (§ 2). Even supposing you point to synthetic judgments (such as the principles of sufficient reason, which you have never proved, as you ought to, from pure reason *a priori,* though we gladly concede its truth), you lapse, when you try to use them for your principal purpose, into such inadmissible and uncertain assertions that in all ages one metaphysics has contradicted another, either in its assertions or their proofs, and thus has itself destroyed its own claim to lasting assent. Nay, the very attempts to set up such a science are the main cause of the early appearance of scepticism, a way of thinking in which reason treats itself with such violence that it could never have arisen save from complete despair of ever satisfying our most important aspirations. For long before men began to inquire into nature methodically, they consulted abstract reason, which had to some extent been exercised by means of ordinary experience; for reason is ever present, while laws of nature must usually be discovered with labor. So metaphysics floated to the surface, like foam, which dissolved the moment it was scooped off. But immediately there appeared a new supply on the surface, to be ever eagerly gathered up by some; while others, instead of seeking in the depths the cause of the phenomenon, thought they showed their wisdom by ridiculing the idle labor of their neighbors.

Weary therefore of dogmatism, which teaches us nothing, and 274 of scepticism, which does not even promise us anything, not even to rest in permitted ignorance; disquieted by the importance of knowledge so much needed; and, lastly, rendered suspicious by long experience of all knowledge which we believe we possess or which offers itself under the title of pure reason— we have left but one critical question upon whose answer depends our future conduct, viz., *is metaphysics at all possible?* But this question must be answered not by sceptical objections to the asseverations of some actual system of metaphysics (for we do not as yet admit such a thing to exist), but from the conception, as yet only problematic, of a science of this sort.

In the *Critique of Pure Reason* I have treated this question synthetically, by making inquiries into pure reason itself and endeavoring in this source to determine the elements as well as the laws of its pure use according to principles. The task is difficult and requires a resolute reader to penetrate by degrees into a system based on no data except reason itself, and which therefore seeks, without resting upon any fact, to unfold knowledge from its original germs. These *Prolegomena,* however, are designed for preparatory exercises; they are intended to point out what must be done in order to make a science actual if it is possible, rather than to expound it. They must therefore rest upon 275 something already known as trustworthy, from which we can set out with confidence and ascend to sources as yet unknown, the discovery of which will not only explain to us what we knew but exhibit a sphere of many cognitions which all spring from the same sources. The method of such *Prolegomena*, especially of those designed as a preparation for future metaphysics, is consequently analytical.

But it happens, fortunately, that though we cannot assume metaphysics to be an actual science, we can say with confidence that certain pure *a priori* synthetic cognitions are actual and given, namely, pure mathematics and pure physics; for both contain propositions which are everywhere recognized as apodeictically certain, partly by mere reason, partly by universal agreement from experience, and yet as independent of experience. We have therefore some, at least uncontested, synthetic knowledge *a priori*, and need not ask *whether* it be possible (for it is actual) but *how* it is possible, in order that we may deduce from the principle which makes the given knowledge possible the possibility of all the rest.

§ 5. The General Question: How is Cognition from Pure Reason Possible?

We have above learned the significant distinction between analytic and synthetic judgments. The possibility of analytic propositions was easily comprehended, being entirely founded on the principle of contradiction. The possibility of synthetic *a posteriori* judgments, of those which are gathered from experience, also requires no special explanation; for experience is nothing but a continual joining together (synthesis) of perceptions. There remain therefore only synthetic propositions *a priori*, of which the possibility must be sought or investigated, because they must depend upon other principles than that of contradiction.

276   But here we need not first establish the possibility of such propositions so as to ask whether they are possible. For there are enough of them which indeed are of undoubted certainty, and as our present method is analytical, we shall start from the fact that such synthetic but purely rational cognition actually exists; but

we must now inquire into the ground of this possibility and ask
how such cognition is possible, in order that we may, from the
principles of its possibility, be enabled to determine the conditions of its use, its sphere, and its limits. The proper problem
upon which all depends, when expressed with scholastic precision, is therefore:

How are synthetic propositions *a priori* possible?

For the sake of popularity I have above expressed this problem somewhat differently, as an inquiry into purely rational cognition, which I could do for once without detriment to the
desired insight, because, as we have only to do here with metaphysics and its sources, the reader will, I hope, after the foregoing remarks, keep in mind that when we speak of purely rational
cognition we do not mean analytic but synthetic cognition.[6]

Metaphysics stands or falls with the solution of this problem;
its very existence depends upon it. Let anyone make metaphysical assertions with ever so much plausibility, let him overwhelm   277
us with conclusions; but if he has not first been able to answer
this question satisfactorily, I have the right to say: this is all vain,
baseless philosophy and false wisdom. You speak through pure
reason and claim, as it were, to create cognitions *a priori* not only
by dissecting given concepts, but also by asserting connections
which do not rest upon the principle of contradiction, and which
you believe you conceive quite independently of all experience;
how do you arrive at this, and how will you justify such pretensions? An appeal to the consent of the common sense of
mankind cannot be allowed, for that is a witness whose authority

6. It is unavoidable that as knowledge advances certain expressions which
have become classical after having been used since the infancy of science will
be found inadequate and unsuitable, and a newer and more appropriate application of the terms will give rise to confusion. [This is the case with the term
"analytic."] The analytical method, insofar as it is opposed to the synthetical,
is very different from an aggregate of analytic propositions. It signifies only that
we start from what is sought, as if it were given, and ascend to the only conditions under which it is possible. In this method we often use nothing but synthetic propositions, as in mathematical analysis, and it were better to term it
the regressive method, in contradistinction to the synthetical or progressive. A
principal part of logic too is distinguished by the name of analytic, which here
signifies the logic of truth in contrast to dialectic, without considering whether
the cognitions belonging to it are analytic or synthetic.

depends merely upon rumor. Says Horace:

Quodcunque ostendis mihi sic, incredulus odi.[7]

The answer to this question is as indispensable as it is difficult; and though the principal reason that it was not attempted long ago is that the possibility of the question never occurred to anybody, there is yet another reason, viz., that a satisfactory answer to this one question requires a much more persistent, profound, and painstaking reflection than the most diffuse work on metaphysics, which on its first appearance promised immortality to its author. And every intelligent reader, when he carefully reflects what this problem requires, must at first be struck with its difficulty, and would regard it as insoluble and even impossible did there not actually exist pure synthetic cognitions *a priori.* This actually happened to David Hume, though he did not conceive the question in its entire universality as is done here and as must be done, if the answer is to be decisive for all metaphysics. For how is it possible, says that acute man, that when a concept is given me I can go beyond it and connect with it another which is not contained in it, in such a manner as if the latter *necessarily* belonged to the former? Nothing but experience can furnish us with such connections (thus he concluded from the difficulty which he took to be an impossibility), and all that vaunted necessity or, what is the same thing, all cognition assumed to be *a priori* is nothing but a long habit of accepting something as true, and hence of mistaking subjective necessity for objective.

278   Should my reader complain of the difficulty and the trouble which I occasion him in the solution of this problem, he is at liberty to solve it himself in an easier way. Perhaps he will then feel under obligation to the person who has undertaken for him a labor of so profound research and will rather be surprised at the facility with which, considering the nature of the subject, the solution has been attained. Yet it has cost years of work to solve the problem in its whole universality (using the term in the mathematical sense, viz., for that which is sufficient for all cases), and finally to exhibit it in the analytical form, as the reader will find it here.

7. ["Whatever is shown me thus, I do not believe and do hate."] *Epistle* II, 3, 188.

All metaphysicians are therefore solemnly and legally suspended from their occupations till they shall have satisfactorily answered the question: *How are synthetic cognitions a priori possible?* For the answer contains the only credentials which they must show when they have anything to offer us in the name of pure reason. But if they do not possess these credentials, they can expect nothing else of reasonable people, who have been deceived so often, than to be dismissed without further ado.

If they, on the other hand, desire to carry on their business, not as a science, but as an art of wholesome persuasion suitable for the common sense of man, they cannot in fairness be prevented from pursuing this trade. They will then speak the modest language of a rational belief; they will grant that they are not allowed even to conjecture, far less to know, anything which lies beyond the bounds of all possible experience, but only to assume (not for speculative use, which they must abandon, but for practical use only) the existence of something that is possible and even indispensable for the guidance of the understanding and of the will in life. In this manner alone can they be called useful and wise men, and the more so as they renounce the title of metaphysicians. For the latter profess to be speculative philosophers; and since, when judgments *a priori* are under discussion, poor probabilities cannot be admitted (for what is declared to be known *a priori* is thereby announced as necessary), such men cannot be permitted to play with conjectures, but their assertions must be either science or else nothing at all. 279

It may be said that the entire transcendental philosophy, which necessarily precedes all metaphysics, is nothing but the complete solution of the problem here propounded, in systematic order and completeness, and that we have hitherto never had any transcendental philosophy. For what goes by its name is properly a part of metaphysics, whereas the former science has first to settle the possibility of the latter and must therefore precede all metaphysics. And it is not surprising that when a whole science, deprived of all help from other sciences and consequently in itself quite new, is required to answer a single question satisfactorily, we should find the answer troublesome and difficult, nay, even shrouded in obscurity.

As we now proceed to this solution according to the analytical method, in which we assume that such cognitions from pure reason actually exist, we can only appeal to two sciences of theoretical cognition (which alone is under consideration here), namely, pure mathematics and pure natural science. For these alone can exhibit to us objects in intuition and consequently (if there should occur in them a cognition *a priori*) can show the truth or conformity of the cognition to the object *in concreto*, that is, its actuality, from which we could proceed to the ground of its possibility by the analytical method. This facilitates our work greatly, for here universal considerations are not only applied to facts, but even start from them, while in a synthetic procedure they must strictly be derived *in abstracto* from concepts.

But in order to ascend from these actual and, at the same time, well-grounded pure cognitions *a priori* to a possible cognition of the kind that we are seeking, viz., to metaphysics as a science, we must comprehend that which occasions it, namely, the mere natural (though not above suspicion as to its truth) cognition *a priori* which lies at the foundation of that science, the elaboration of which without any critical investigation of its possibility is commonly called metaphysics. In a word, we must comprehend the natural conditions of such a science as a part of our inquiry, and thus the transcendental problem will be gradually answered by a division into four questions:

> *1. How is pure mathematics possible?*
> *2. How is pure natural science possible?*
> *3. How is metaphysics in general possible?*
> *4. How is metaphysics as a science possible?*

It may be seen that the solution of these problems, though chiefly designed to exhibit the essential content of the *Critique*, has yet something peculiar, which for itself alone deserves attention. This is the search for the sources of given sciences in reason itself, so that its faculty of knowing something *a priori* may by its own deeds be investigated and measured. By this procedure these sciences gain, if not with regard to their contents, yet as to their proper use; and while they throw light on the higher question concerning their common origin, they give, at the same time, an occasion for better explaining their own nature.

280

FIRST PART OF THE
MAIN TRANSCENDENTAL QUESTION

How is Pure Mathematics Possible?

§ 6. Here is a great and established branch of knowledge, encompassing even now a wonderfully large domain and promising an unlimited extension in the future, and carrying with it thoroughly apodeictical certainty, i.e., absolute necessity, which therefore rests upon no empirical grounds. Consequently it is a pure product of reason, and moreover is thoroughly synthetic. [Here the question arises:] "How then is it possible for human reason to produce such cognition entirely *a priori?*" Does not this faculty [which produces mathematics], as it neither is nor can be based upon experience, presuppose some ground of cognition *a priori*, which lies deeply hidden but which might reveal itself by these its effects, if their first beginnings were but diligently ferreted out?

§ 7. But we find that all mathematical cognition has this   281 peculiarity: it must first exhibit its concept in intuition, and do so *a priori*, in an intuition that is not empirical but pure. Without this mathematics cannot take a single step; hence its judgments are always *intuitive;* whereas philosophy must be satisfied with *discursive* judgments from mere concepts, and though it may illustrate its apodeictic doctrines through intuition, can never derive them from it. This observation on the nature of mathematics gives us a clue to the first and highest condition of its possibility, which is that some pure intuition must form its basis, in which all its concepts can be exhibited or constructed, *in concreto* and yet *a priori*.[8] If we can discover this pure intuition and its possibility, we may thence easily explain how synthetic propositions *a priori* are possible in pure mathematics, and consequently

8. [See *Critique of Pure Reason*, B 741.]

how this science itself is possible. For just as empirical intuition
[viz., sense-perception] enables us without difficulty to enlarge
the concept which we frame of an object of intuition by new
predicates which intuition itself presents synthetically in experience, so pure intuition also does likewise, only with this
difference: that in the latter case the synthetic judgment is *a
priori* certain and apodeictic, in the former only *a posteriori* and
empirically certain, because the *a posteriori* case contains only
that which occurs in contingent empirical intuition, but the *a
priori* case contains that which must necessarily be discovered in
pure intuition. Here intuition, being an intuition *a priori,* is in-
separably joined with the concept before all experience or particular perception.

§ 8. But with this step our perplexity seems rather to increase
than to lessen. For the question now is, "How is it possible to
282 intuit anything *a priori?*" An intuition is such a representation as
would immediately depend upon the presence of the object.
Hence it seems impossible to intuit anything *a priori* originally,
because intuition would in that event have to take place without
either a former or a present object to refer to, and hence could
not be intuition. Concepts indeed are such that we can easily
form some of them *a priori,* viz., such as contain nothing but the
thought of an object in general; and we need not find ourselves
in an immediate relation to the object. Take, for instance, the
concepts of quantity, of cause, etc. But even these require, in
order to be meaningful and significant, certain concrete use—
that is, an application to some intuition by which an object of
them is given us. But how can the intuition of the object precede
the object itself?

§ 9. If our intuition had to be of such a nature as to represent
things as they are in themselves, there would not be any intuition *a priori,* but intuition would be always empirical. For I can
only know what is contained in the object in itself if it is present
and given to me. It is indeed even then inconceivable how the
intuition of a present thing should make me know this thing as it
is in itself, as its properties cannot migrate into my faculty of representation. But even if this possibility be granted, an intuition
of that sort would not take place *a priori,* that is, before the
object were presented to me; for without this latter fact no

ground of a relation between my representation and the object can be conceived, unless it rested on inspiration. Therefore in one way only can my intuition anticipate the actuality of the object, and be a cognition *a priori*, viz., *if my intuition contains nothing but the form of sensibility, which in me as subject precedes all the actual impressions through which I am affected by objects.* For that objects of sense can only be intuited according to this form of sensibility I can know *a priori.* Hence it follows that propositions which concern this form of sensuous intuition only are possible and valid for objects of the senses; as also, conversely, that intuitions which are possible *a priori* can never concern any other things than objects of our senses.

§ 10. Accordingly, it is only the form of sensuous intuition by   **283** which we can intuit things *a priori*, but by which we can know objects only as they *appear* to us (to our senses), not as they are in themselves; and this assumption is absolutely necessary if synthetic propositions *a priori* be granted as possible or if, in case they actually occur, their possibility is to be conceived and determined beforehand.

Now, the intuitions which pure mathematics lays at the foundation of all its cognitions and judgments which appear at once apodeictic and necessary are space and time. For mathematics must first present all its concepts in intuition, and pure mathematics in pure intuition, i.e., it must construct them. If it proceeded in any other way, it would be impossible to make a single step; for mathematics proceeds, not analytically by dissection of concepts, but synthetically, and if pure intuition be wanting there is nothing in which the matter for synthetic judgments *a priori* can be given. Geometry is based upon the pure intuition of space. Arithmetic attains its concepts of numbers by the successive addition of units in time, and pure mechanics especially can attain its concepts of motion only by employing the representation of time. Both representations, however, are merely intuitions; for if we omit from the empirical intuitions of bodies and their alterations (motion) everything empirical, i.e., belonging to sensation, space and time still remain, and are therefore pure intuitions that lie *a priori* at the basis of the empirical. Hence they can never be omitted; but at the same time, by their being pure intuitions *a priori*, they prove that they are mere forms of our sensibility, which must precede all empirical intuition, i.e., perception of actual objects, and in conformity with which objects can be known *a priori* but only as they appear to us.

§ 11. The problem of the present section is therefore solved. Pure mathematics, as synthetic cognition *a priori,* is possible only by referring to no other objects than those of the senses. At the basis of their empirical intuition lies a pure intuition (of space and time), which is *a priori.* This is possible because the latter intuition is nothing but the mere form of sensibility, which precedes the actual appearance of the objects, since in fact it makes them possible. Yet this faculty of intuiting *a priori* concerns not the matter of the appearance (that is, the sensation in it, for this constitutes what is empirical), but its form, viz., space and time. Should any man venture to doubt that both are not determinations of things in themselves but are merely determinations of their relation to sensibility, I should be glad to know how it can be possible to know *a priori* how their intuition will be characterized before we have any acquaintance with them and before they are presented to us. Such, however, is the case with space and time. But this is quite conceivable as soon as both count for nothing more than formal conditions of our sensibility, while the objects count merely as appearance; for then the form of the appearance, i.e., pure intuition, can by all means be represented as proceeding from ourselves, that is, *a priori.*

§ 12. In order to add something by way of illustration and confirmation, we need only watch the ordinary and unavoidably necessary procedure of geometers. All proofs of the complete congruence of two given figures (where the one can in every respect be substituted for the other) ultimately come down to the fact that they may be made to coincide. This is evidently nothing but a synthetic proposition resting upon immediate intuition; and this intuition must be pure and given *a priori,* else the proposition could not hold as apodeictically certain but would have empirical certainty only. In that case it could only be said that it is always found to be so and holds good only as far as our perception reaches. That complete space (which is not itself the boundary of another space) has three dimensions and that space in general cannot have more is based on the proposition that not more than three lines can intersect at right angles in one point.

284

This proposition cannot at all be shown from concepts, but rests   285
immediately on intuition, and indeed on pure intuition *a priori*
because it is apodeictically certain. That we can require a line to
be drawn to infinity (*in indefinitum*) or that a series of changes
(for example, spaces traversed by motion) shall be infinitely
continued presupposes a representation of space and time,
which can only attach to intuition, namely, so far as it in itself is
bounded by nothing, for from concepts it could never be inferred. Consequently, the basis of mathematics actually is pure
intuitions, which make its synthetic and apodeictically valid
propositions possible. Hence our transcendental deduction of
the concepts of space and of time explains at the same time the
possibility of pure mathematics. Without some such deduction
its truth may be granted, but its existence could by no means be
understood, and we must assume "that everything which can be
given to our senses (to the external senses in space and to the
internal sense in time) is intuited by us as it appears to us, not as
it is in itself."

§ 13. Those who cannot yet rid themselves of the notion that
space and time are actual qualities inherent in things in themselves may exercise their acumen on the following paradox.
When they have in vain attempted its solution and are free from
prejudices at least for a few moments, they will suspect that the
reduction of space and time to mere forms of our sensuous
intuition may perhaps be well founded.

If two things are quite equal in all respects as much as can be
ascertained by all means possible, quantitatively and qualitative-
ly, it must follow that the one can in all cases and under all circumstances replace the other, and this substitution would not
occasion the least recognizable difference. This in fact is true of
plane figures in geometry; but some spherical figures exhibit,
notwithstanding a complete internal agreement, such a
difference in their external relation that the one figure cannot
possibly be put in the place of the other. For instance, two
spherical triangles on opposite hemispheres which have an arc of
the equator as their common base may be quite equal, both as   286
regards sides and angles, so that nothing is to be found in either,
if it be described for itself alone and completed, that would not
equally be applicable to both; and yet the one cannot be put in

the place of the other (on the opposite hemisphere). Here, then, is an internal difference between the two triangles; this difference our understanding cannot show to be internal but only manifests itself by external relations in space. But I shall adduce examples, taken from common life, that are more obvious still.

What can be more similar in every respect and in every part more alike to my hand and to my ear than their images in a mirror? And yet I cannot put such a hand as is seen in the mirror in the place of its original; for if this is a right hand, that in the mirror is a left one, and the image or reflection of the right ear is a left one, which never can serve as a substitute for the other. There are in this case no internal differences which our understanding could determine by thinking alone. Yet the differences are internal as the senses teach, for, notwithstanding their complete equality and similarity, the left hand cannot be enclosed in the same bounds as the right one (they are not congruent); the glove of one hand cannot be used for the other. What is the solution? These objects are not representations of things as they are in themselves, and as some pure understanding would cognize them, but sensuous intuitions, that is, appearances, whose possibility rests upon the relation of certain things unknown in themselves to something else, viz., to our sensibility. Space is the form of the external intuition of this sensibility, and the internal determination of any space is possible only by the determination of its external relation to the whole of space, of which it is a part (in other words, by its relation to external sense). That is to say, the part is possible only through the whole, which is never the case with things in themselves as objects of the mere understanding, but can well be the case with mere appearances. Hence the difference between similar and equal things which are not congruent (for instance, helices winding in opposite ways) cannot be made intelligible by any concept, but only by the relation to the right and the left hands, which immediately refers to intuition.

REMARK I

287   Pure mathematics, and especially pure geometry, can only

have objective reality on condition that it refers merely to objects of sense. But in regard to the latter the principle holds good that our sense representation is not a representation of things in themselves, but of the way in which they appear to us. Hence it follows that the propositions of geometry are not determinations of a mere creation of our poetic imagination, which could therefore not be referred with assurance to actual objects; but rather that they are necessarily valid of space, and consequently of all that may be found in space, because space is nothing but the form of all external appearances, and it is this form alone in which objects of sense can be given to us. Sensibility, the form of which is the basis of geometry, is that upon which the possibility of external appearance depends. Therefore these appearances can never contain anything but what geometry prescribes to them. It would be quite otherwise if the senses were so constituted as to represent objects as they are in themselves. For then it would not by any means follow from the representation of space, which with all its properties serves the geometer as an *a priori* foundation, that this foundation together with what is inferred from it must be so in nature. The space of the geometer would be considered a mere fiction, and it would not be credited with objective validity because we cannot see how things must of necessity agree with an image of them which we make spontaneously and previous to our acquaintance with them. But if this image, or rather this formal intuition, is the essential property of our sensibility by means of which alone objects are given to us, and if this sensibility represents not things in themselves but their appearances, then we shall easily comprehend, and at the same time indisputably prove, that all external objects of our world of sense must necessarily coincide in the most rigorous way with the propositions of geometry. This is so because sensibility by means of its form of external intuition (space), with which the geometer is concerned, makes those objects possible as mere appearances. It will always remain a remarkable phenomenon in the history of philosophy that there was a time when even mathematicians who at the same time were philosophers began to doubt, not of the correctness of their geometrical propositions so far as they merely concerned space, but of their objective validity and the applicability to 288 nature of this concept itself and all its geometrical determinations. They showed much concern whether a line in nature might not consist of physical points, and consequently that true space in the object might consist of simple parts, while the space which the geometer has in his mind cannot be such. They did not recognize that this thought space renders possible the physical space, i.e., the extension of matter itself, and that this pure space is not at all a quality of things in themselves but a form of our sensuous faculty of representation, and that furthermore all objects in space are mere appearances, i.e., not things in themselves but representations of our sensuous intuition. But such is the case, for the space of the geometer is exactly the form of sensuous intuition which we find *a priori* in us, and contains the ground of the possibility of all external appearances (according to their form); and the latter must necessarily and most precisely agree with the propositions of the geometer, which he draws not from any fictitious concept but from the subjective basis of all external appearances, viz., sensibility itself. In this and no other way can geometry be made secure as to the undoubted objective reality of its propositions against all the chicaneries of a shallow metaphysics, however strange this may seem to a metaphysics that does not go back to the sources of its concepts.

REMARK II

Whatever is given us as object must be given us in intuition. All our intuition, however, takes place only by means of the senses; the understanding intuits nothing but only reflects. And as we have just shown that the senses never and in no manner enable us to know things in themselves, but only their appearances, which are mere representations of the sensibility, we conclude that "all bodies, together with the space in which they are, must be considered nothing but mere representations in us, and exist nowhere but in our thoughts." Now is not this manifest idealism?

Idealism consists in the assertion that there are none but thinking beings; all other things which we believe are perceived in intuition are nothing but representations in the thinking beings, to which no object external to them in fact corresponds.

On the contrary, I say that things as objects of our senses existing outside us are given, but we know nothing of what they may be in themselves, knowing only their appearances, i.e., the representations which they cause in us by affecting our senses. Consequently, I grant by all means that there are bodies without us, that is, things which, though quite unknown to us as to what they are in themselves, we yet know by the representations which their influence on our sensibility procures us, and which we call bodies. This word merely means the appearance of the thing, which is unknown to us but is not therefore less real. Can this be termed idealism? It is the very contrary.

Long before Locke's time, but assuredly since him, it has been generally assumed and granted without detriment to the actual existence of external things that many of their predicates may be said to belong, not to the things in themselves, but to their appearances, and to have no proper existence outside our representation. Heat, color, and taste, for instance, are of this kind. Now, if I go further and, for weighty reasons, rank as mere appearances also the remaining qualities of bodies, which are called primary—such as extension, place, and, in general, space, with all that which belongs to it (impenetrability or materiality, shape, etc.)—no one in the least can adduce the reason of its being inadmissible. As little as the man who admits colors not to be properties of the object in itself but only to be modifications of the sense of sight should on that account be called an idealist, so little can my doctrine be named idealistic merely because I find that more, nay, *all the properties which constitute the intuition of a body belong merely to its appearance.* The existence of the thing that appears is thereby not destroyed, as in genuine idealism, but it is only shown that we cannot possibly know it by the senses as it is in itself.

I should be glad to know what my assertions must be in order to avoid all idealism. Undoubtedly, I should say that the representation of space is not only perfectly conformable to the relation which our sensibility has to objects—that I have said—but 290 that it is completely like the object—an assertion in which I can find as little meaning as if I said that the sensation of red has a similarity to the property of cinnabar which excites this sensation in me.

REMARK III

Hence we may at once dismiss an easily foreseen but futile objection, "that by our admitting the ideality of space and of time the whole sensible world would be turned into mere illusion." After all philosophical insight into the nature of sensuous cognition was spoiled by making the sensibility merely a confused mode of representation, according to which we still know things as they are, but without being able to reduce everything in this our representation to a clear consciousness; whereas on the contrary proof is offered by us that sensibility consists, not in this logical distinction of clearness and obscurity, but in the genetic one of the origin of cognition itself. For sensuous perception represents things not at all as they are, but only the mode in which they affect our senses; and consequently by sensuous perception appearances only, and not things themselves, are given to the understanding for reflection. After this necessary correction, an objection rises from an unpardonable and almost intentional misconception, as if my doctrine turned all the things of the world of sense into mere illusion.

When an appearance is given us, we are still quite free as to how we should judge the matter. The appearance depends upon the senses, but the judgment upon the understanding; and the only question is whether in the determination of the object there is truth or not. But the difference between truth and dreaming is not ascertained by the nature of the representations which are referred to objects (for they are the same in both cases), but by their connection according to those rules which determine the coherence of the representations in the concept of an object, and by ascertaining whether they can subsist together in experience or not. And it is not the fault of the appearances if our cognition takes illusion for truth, i.e., if the intuition, by which an object is given us, is taken for the concept of the thing or even of its existence, which the understanding only can think. The senses represent to us the paths of the planets as now progressive, now retrogressive; and therein is neither falsehood nor truth, because as long as we hold this to be nothing but appearance we do not judge of the objective nature of their motion. But as a false judgment may easily arise when the understanding is not on its guard against this subjective mode of representation being considered objective, we say they appear to move backward; it is not the senses however which must be charged with the illusion, but the understanding, whose province alone it is to make an objective judgment on appearances.

Thus, even if we did not at all reflect on the origin of our representations, whenever we connect our intuitions of sense (whatever they may contain) in space and in time, according to the rules of the coherence of all cognition in experience, illusion or truth will arise according as we are negligent or careful. It is merely a question of the use of sensuous representations in the understanding, and not of their origin. In the same way, if I consider all the representations of the senses, together with their form, space and time, to be nothing but appearances, and space and time to be a mere form of the sensibility, which is not to be met with in objects out of it, and if I make use of these representations in reference to possible experience only, there is nothing in my regarding them as appearances that can lead astray or cause illusion. For all that, they can correctly cohere according to rules of truth in experience. Thus all the propositions of geometry hold good of space as well as of all the objects of the senses, consequently, of all possible experience, whether I consider space as a mere form of the sensibility or as something adhering to the things themselves. In the former case, however, I comprehend how I can know *a priori* these propositions concerning all the objects of external intuition. Otherwise, everything else as regards all possible experience remains just as if I had not departed from the ordinary view.

But if I venture to go beyond all possible experience with my concepts of space and time, which I cannot refrain from doing if I proclaim them qualities inherent in things in themselves (for what should prevent me from letting them hold good of the same things, even though my senses might be different, and unsuited to them?), then a grave error may arise due to illusion, in which I proclaim to be universally valid what is merely a subjective condition of the intuition of things and certain only for all objects of sense, viz., for all possible experience; I would refer this condition to things in themselves, and not limit it to the conditions of experience.

My doctrine of the ideality of space and of time, therefore, far from reducing the whole sensible world to mere illusion, is the only means of securing the application of one of the most important cognitions (that which mathematics propounds *a priori*) to actual objects and of preventing its being regarded as mere illusion. For without this observation it would be quite impossible to make out whether the intuitions of space and time, which we borrow from no experience and which yet lie in our representation *a priori*, are not mere phantasms of our brain to which no objects correspond, at least not adequately; and, consequently, whether we have been able to show geometry's unquestionable validity with regard to all the objects of the sensible world just because they are mere appearances.

Secondly, though these my principles make appearances of the representations of the senses, they are so far from turning the truth of experience into mere illusion that they are rather the only means of preventing the transcendental illusion, by which metaphysics has been deceived hitherto and misled into childish efforts of catching at bubbles, because appearances, which are mere representations, were taken for things in themselves. Here originated the remarkable event of the antinomy of reason, which I shall mention later on and which is cancelled by the single observation that appearance, as long as it is employed in experience, produces truth, but the moment it transgresses the bounds of experience, and consequently becomes transcendent, produces nothing but illusion [see §§ 50–54 below].

293   Inasmuch, therefore, as I leave to things as we obtain them by the senses their actuality and only limit our sensuous intuition of these things to this—that it represents in no respect, not even in the pure intuitions of space and of time, anything more than mere appearance of those things, but never their constitution in themselves—so is this position of mine not a sweeping illusion invented by me for nature. My protestation, too, against all charges of idealism is so valid and clear as even to seem superfluous, were there not incompetent judges who, while they would have an old name for every deviation from their perverse though common opinion and never judge of the spirit of philosophic nomenclature, but cling to the letter only, are ready to put their own conceits in the place of well-defined concepts, and

thereby deform and distort them. I have myself given this my theory the name of transcendental idealism, but that cannot authorize anyone to confound it either with the empirical idealism of Descartes (indeed, his was only an insoluble problem, owing to which he thought every one at liberty to deny the existence of the corporeal world because it could never be proved satisfactorily), or with the mystical and visionary idealism of Berkeley (against which and other similar phantasms, our *Critique* contains the proper antidote). My idealism concerns not the existence of things (the doubting of which, however, constitutes idealism in the ordinary sense), since it never came into my head to doubt it; but it concerns the sensuous representation of things, to which space and time especially belong. Regarding space and time and, consequently, regarding all appearances in general, I have only shown that they are neither things (but are mere modes of representation) nor are they determinations belonging to things in themselves. But the word "transcendental," which for me never means a reference of our cognition to things, but only to our faculty of cognition, was meant to obviate this misconception. Yet rather than give further occasion to it by this word, I now retract it and desire this idealism of mine to be called "critical." But if it be really an objectionable idealism to convert actual things (not appearances) into mere representations, by what name shall we call that which, conversely, changes mere representations into things? It may, I think, be called *dreaming* idealism, in contradistinction to the former, which may be called *visionary* idealism, both of which are to be 294 refuted by my transcendental, or better, *critical* idealism.

SECOND PART OF THE
MAIN TRANSCENDENTAL QUESTION

How is Pure Natural Science Possible?

§ 14. *Nature* is the *existence* of things, so far as it is determined according to universal laws Should nature signify the existence of things in themselves, we could never cognize it either *a priori* or *a posteriori*. Not *a priori*, for how can we know what belongs to things in themselves, since this never can be done by the dissection of our concepts (in analytic judgments)? For I do not want to know what is contained in my concept of a thing (for that belongs to its logical being), but what in the actuality of the thing is superadded to my concept and by what the thing itself is determined in its existence outside the concept. My understanding and the conditions on which alone it can connect the determinations of things in their existence do not prescribe any rule to things in themselves; these do not conform to my understanding, but it would have to conform to them; they would therefore have to be first given to me in order to gather these determinations from them, wherefore they would not be cognized *a priori*.

A cognition of the nature of things in themselves *a posteriori* would be equally impossible. For if experience is to teach us laws to which the existence of things is subject, these laws, if they refer to things in themselves, would have to refer to them of necessity even outside our experience. But experience teaches us what exists and how it exists, but never that it must necessarily exist so and not otherwise. Experience therefore can never teach us the nature of things in themselves.

§ 15. We nevertheless actually possess a pure natural science in which are propounded, *a priori* and with all the necessity requisite to apodeictic propositions, laws to which nature is subject. I need only call to witness that propaedeutic to natural

295

38

knowledge which, under the title of universal natural science,[9] precedes all physics (which is founded upon empirical principles). In it we have mathematics applied to appearances, and also merely discursive principles (from concepts),[10] which constitute the philosophical part of the pure cognition of nature. But there is much in it which is not quite pure and independent of empirical sources, such as the concept of *motion*, that of *impenetrability* (upon which the empirical concept of matter rests), that of *inertia*, and many others, which prevent its being called a quite pure [transcendental] natural science. Besides, it only refers to objects of the external senses, and therefore does not give an example of a universal natural science in the strict sense; for such a science must bring nature in general, whether it regards the object of the external senses or that of the internal sense (the object of physics as well as psychology), under universal laws. But among the principles of this universal physics there are a few which actually have the required universality; for instance, the propositions that "substance is permanent," and that "every event is determined by a cause according to constant laws," etc. These are actually universal laws of nature, which subsist completely *a priori*. There is then in fact a pure [transcendental] natural science, and the question arises: how is it possible?

§ 16. The word *nature* assumes yet another meaning, which determines the object, whereas in the former sense it only denotes the conformity to law of the determinations of the existence of things generally. Nature considered *materialiter* is the *totality of all objects of experience*. And with this only are we now concerned; for, besides, things which can never be objects of experience, if they were to be cognized as to their nature, would oblige us to have recourse to concepts whose meaning could never be given *in concreto* (by any example of possible experience). Consequently, we would have to form for ourselves a list of concepts of their nature, the reality whereof (i.e., whether they actually referred to objects or were mere creations of **296** thought) could never be determined. The cognition of what can-

9. [Contained in Kant's *Metaphysical Foundations of Natural Science* (1786)]

10. [Rather than intuitive principles, like mathematics]

not be an object of experience would be hyperphysical, and with things hyperphysical we are here not concerned, but only with the cognition of nature, the actuality of which can be confirmed by experience, though this cognition is possible *a priori* and precedes all experience.

§ 17. The formal aspect of nature in this narrower sense is therefore the conformity to law of all the objects of experience and, so far as it is cognized *a priori*, their necessary conformity. But it has just been shown that the laws of nature can never be cognized *a priori* in objects so far as they are considered, not in reference to possible experience, but as things in themselves. And our inquiry here extends, not to things in themselves (the properties of which we pass by), but to things as objects of possible experience, and the totality of these is properly what we here call nature. And now I ask, when the possibility of cognition of nature *a priori* is in question, whether it is better to arrange the problem thus: how can we cognize *a priori* that things as objects of experience necessarily conform to law? or thus: how is it possible to cognize *a priori* the necessary conformity to law of experience itself as regards all its objects generally?

Closely considered, the solution of the question represented in either way amounts, with regard to the pure cognition of nature (which is the point of the question at issue), entirely to the same thing. For the subjective laws, under which alone an empirical cognition of things is possible, hold good of these things as objects of possible experience (not as things in themselves, which are not considered here). Either of the following statements means quite the same: a judgment of perception can never rank as experience without the law that, whenever an event is observed, it is always referred to some antecedent, which it follows according to a universal rule; or else, everything of which experience teaches that it happens must have a cause.

297   It is, however, more convenient to choose the first formula. For we can *a priori* and before all given objects have a cognition of those conditions on which alone experience of them is possible, but never of the laws to which things may in themselves be subject, without reference to possible experience. We cannot, therefore, study the nature of things *a priori* otherwise than by investigating the conditions and the universal (though sub-

jective) laws, under which alone such a cognition as experience (as to mere form) is possible, and we determine accordingly the possibility of things as objects of experience. For if I should choose the second formula and seek the *a priori* conditions under which nature as an object of experience is possible, I might easily fall into error and fancy that I was speaking of nature as a thing in itself, and then move round in endless circles, in a vain search for laws concerning things of which nothing is given me.

Accordingly, we shall here be concerned merely with experience and the universal conditions of its possibility, which are given *a priori*. Thence we shall determine nature as the whole object of all possible experience. I think it will be understood that I here do not mean the rules of the observation of a nature that is already given, for these already presuppose experience. I do not mean how (through experience) we can study the laws of nature; for these would not then be laws *a priori* and would yield us no pure natural science; but [I mean to ask] how the conditions *a priori* of the possibility of experience are at the same time the sources from which all the universal laws of nature must be derived.

§ 18. In the first place we must state that while all judgments of experience are empirical (i.e., have their ground in immediate sense-perception), yet conversely, all empirical judgments are not therefore judgments of experience; but, besides the empirical, and in general besides what is given to sensuous intuition, special concepts must yet be superadded—concepts which have their origin quite *a priori* in the pure understanding, and under which every perception must be first of all subsumed and then by their means changed into experience.

Empirical judgments, so far as they have objective validity, are   298 *judgments of experience;* but those which are only subjectively valid I name mere *judgments of perception*. The latter require no pure concept of the understanding, but only the logical connection of perception in a thinking subject. But the former always require, besides the representation of the sensuous intuition, special *concepts originally generated in the understanding*, which make the judgment of experience objectively valid.

All our judgments are at first merely judgments of perception;

they hold good only for us (i.e., for our subject), and we do not till afterwards give them a new reference (to an object) and want that they shall always hold good for us and in the same way for everybody else; for if a judgment agrees with an object, all judgments concerning the same object must likewise agree with one another, and thus the objective validity of the judgment of experience signifies nothing else than its necessary universal validity. And, conversely, if we have reason to hold a judgment to be necessarily universally valid (which never rests on perception, but on the pure concept of the understanding under which the perception is subsumed), we must consider it to be objective also, that is, that it expresses not merely a reference of our perception to a subject, but a quality of the object. For there would be no reason for the judgments of other men necessarily to agree with mine, if it were not the unity of the object to which they all refer and with which they accord; hence they must all agree with one another.

§ 19. Therefore objective validity and necessary universal validity (for everybody) are equivalent concepts, and though we do not know the object in itself, yet when we consider a judgment as universally valid, and hence necessary, we understand it thereby to have objective validity. By this judgment we cognize the object (though it remains unknown as it is in itself) by the universally valid and necessary connection of the given perceptions. As this is the case with all objects of sense, judgments of experience take their objective validity, not from the immediate cognition of the object (which is impossible), but merely from the condition of the universal validity of empirical judgments, which, as already said, never rests upon empirical or, in short, sensuous conditions, but upon a pure concept of the understanding. The object in itself always remains unknown; but when by the concept of the understanding the connection of the representations of the object, which are given by the object to our sensibility, is determined as universally valid, the object is determined by this relation, and the judgment is objective.

To illustrate the matter: when we say, "The room is warm, sugar sweet, and wormwood nasty," [11] we have only subjectively

11. I freely grant that these examples do not represent such judgments of perception as ever could become judgments of experience, even though a con-

valid judgments. I do not at all expect that I or any other person shall always find it as I now do; each of these sentences only expresses a reference of two sensations to the same subject, i.e., myself, and that only in my present state of perception; consequently, they are not intended to be valid of the object. Such are judgments of perception. Judgments of experience are of quite a different nature. What experience teaches me under certain circumstances, it must always teach me and everybody; and its validity is not limited to the subject nor to its state at a particular time. Hence I pronounce all such judgments as being objectively valid. For instance, when I say the air is elastic, this judgment is as yet a judgment of perception only—I do nothing but refer two sensations in my senses to one another. But if I would have it called a judgment of experience, I require this connection to stand under a condition which makes it universally valid. I desire therefore that I and everybody else should always necessarily connect the same perceptions under the same circumstances.

§ 20. We must therefore analyze experience in general in   300
order to see what is contained in this product of the senses and of the understanding, and how the judgment of experience itself is possible. The foundation is the intuition of which I become conscious, i.e., perception *(perceptio),* which pertains merely to the senses. But in the next place, there is judging (which belongs only to the understanding). But this judging may be twofold: first, I may merely compare perceptions and connect them in a consciousness of my state; or, secondly, I may connect them in consciousness in general. The former judgment is merely a judgment of perception and is of subjective validity only; it is merely a connection of perceptions in my mental state, without reference to the object. Hence it is not, as is commonly imagined, enough for experience to compare perceptions and connect

---

cept of the understanding were superadded, because they refer merely to feeling, which everybody knows to be merely subjective and which, of course, can never be attributed to the object and, consequently, never can become objective. I only wished to give here an example of a judgment that is merely subjectively valid, containing no ground for necessary universal validity and thereby for a relation to the object. An example of the judgments of perception which become judgments of experience by superadded concepts of the understanding will be given in the next note.

them in consciousness through judgment; there arises no universal validity and necessity, by virtue of which alone consciousness can become objectively valid and be called experience. Quite another judgment therefore is required before perception can become experience. The given intuition must be subsumed under a concept which determines the form of judging in general with regard to the intuition, connects the empirical consciousness of the intuition in consciousness in general, and thereby procures universal validity for empirical judgments. A concept of this nature is a pure *a priori* concept of the understanding, which does nothing but determine for an intuition the general way in which it can be used for judging. Let the concept be that of cause; then it determines the intuition which is subsumed under it, e.g., that of air, with regard to judging in general, viz., the concept of air as regards its expansion serves in the relation of antecedent to consequent in a hypothetical judgment. The concept of cause accordingly is a pure concept of the understanding, which is totally disparate from all possible perception and only serves to determine the representation contained under it with regard to judging in general, and so to make a universally valid judgment possible.

301   Before, therefore, a judgment of perception can become a judgment of experience, it is requisite that the perception should be subsumed under some such concept of the understanding; for instance, air belongs under the concept of cause, which determines our judgment about it with regard to its expansion as hypothetical.[12] Thereby the expansion of the air is represented, not as merely belonging to the perception of the air in my present state or in several states of mine, or in the state of perception of others, but as belonging to it necessarily. The judgment that air is elastic becomes universally valid and a judgment of experience only because certain judgments precede it which subsume

---

12. As an easier example, we may take the following: when the sun shines on the stone, it grows warm. This judgment, however often I and others may have perceived it, is a mere judgment of perception and contains no necessity; perceptions are only usually conjoined in this manner. But if I say: the sun warms the stone, I add to the perception a concept of the understanding, viz., that of cause, which necessarily connects with the concept of sunshine that of heat, and the synthetic judgment becomes of necessity universally valid, viz., objective, and is converted from a perception into experience.

the intuition of air under the concepts of cause and effect; and they thereby determine the perceptions, not merely as regards one another in me, but as regards the form of judging in general (which is here hypothetical), and in this way they render the empirical judgment universally valid.

If all our synthetic judgments are analyzed so far as they are objectively valid, it will be found that they never consist of mere intuitions connected only (as is commonly supposed) by comparison into a judgment; but that they would be impossible were not a pure concept of the understanding superadded to the concepts abstracted from intuition, under which pure concept these latter concepts are subsumed and in this manner only combined into an objectively valid judgment. Even the judgments of pure mathematics in their simplest axioms are not exempt from this condition. The principle that a straight line is the shortest distance between two points presupposes that the line is subsumed under the concept of quantity, which certainly is no mere intuition but has its seat in the understanding alone and serves to determine the intuition (of the line) with regard to the judgments which may be made about it in respect to the quantity, that is, to plurality (as *judica plurativa*.)[13] For under them it is   302 understood that in a given intuition there is contained a plurality of homogeneous parts.

§ 21. To prove, then, the possibility of experience so far as it rests upon pure *a priori* concepts of the understanding, we must first represent what belongs to judgments in general and the various moments (functions) of the understanding in them, in a complete table. For the pure concepts of the understanding must run parallel to these moments, inasmuch as such concepts are nothing more than concepts of intuitions in general, so far as these are determined by one or other of these moments of judging, in themselves, i.e., necessarily and universally. Hereby also

13. This name seems preferable to the term *particularia*, which is used for these judgments in logic. For the latter already contains the thought that they are not universal. But when I start from unity (in singular judgments) and proceed to totality, I must not [even indirectly and negatively] include any reference to totality. I think plurality merely without totality, and not the exclusion of totality. This is necessary, if the logical moments are to underlie the pure concepts of the understanding. In logical usage one may leave things as they were.

the *a priori* principles of the possibility of all experience, as objectively valid empirical cognition, will be precisely determined. For they are nothing but propositions which subsume all perception (conformably to certain universal conditions of intuition) under those pure concepts of the understanding.

LOGICAL TABLE OF JUDGMENTS

1 *As to Quantity*	2 *As to Quality*
Universal	Affirmative
Particular	Negative
Singular	Infinite

303

3 *As to Relation*	4 *As to Modality*
Categorical	Problematic
Hypothetical	Assertoric
Disjunctive	Apodeictic

TRANSCENDENTAL TABLE OF THE CONCEPTS OF THE UNDERSTANDING

1 *As to Quantity*	2 *As to Quality*
Unity (Measure)	Reality
Plurality (Quantity)	Negation
Totality (Whole)	Limitation

3 *As to Relation*	4 *As to Modality*
Substance	Possibility
Cause	Existence
Community	Necessity

PURE PHYSIOLOGICAL[14] TABLE OF THE UNIVERSAL PRINCIPLES OF NATURAL SCIENCE

1
Axioms of
Intuition

2
Anticipations of
Perception

3
Analogies of
Experience

4
Postulates of
Empirical
Thought in
General

§ 21a. In order to comprise the whole matter in one idea, it is first necessary to remind the reader that we are discussing, not the origin of experience, but what lies in experience. The former pertains to empirical psychology and would even then never be adequately developed without the latter, which belongs to the critique of cognition, and particularly of the understanding. 304

Experience consists of intuitions, which belong to the sensibility, and of judgments, which are entirely a work of the understanding. But the judgments which the understanding makes entirely out of sensuous intuitions are far from being judgments of experience. For in the one case the judgment connects only the perceptions as they are given in sensuous intuition, while in the other the judgments must express what experience in general and not what the mere perception (which possesses only subjective validity) contains. The judgment of experience must therefore add to the sensuous intuition and its logical connection in a judgment (after it has been rendered universal by comparison) something that determines the synthetic judgment as necessary and therefore as universally valid. This can be nothing but that concept which represents the intuition as determined in itself with regard to one form of judgment rather than another, viz., a concept of that synthetic unity of intuitions which can only be represented by a given logical function of judgments.

14. [See last sentence of § 23.]

§ 22. The sum of the matter is this: the business of the senses is to intuit, that of the understanding is to think. But thinking is uniting representations in a consciousness. This unification originates either merely relative to the subject and is contingent and subjective, or it happens absolutely and is necessary or objective. The uniting of representations in a consciousness is judgment. Thinking therefore is the same as judging, or referring representations to judgments in general. Hence judgments are either merely subjective when representations are referred to a consciousness in one subject only and are united in it, or they are objective when they are united in a consciousness in general, that is, necessarily. The logical moments of all judgments are so many possible ways of uniting representations in consciousness. But if they serve as concepts, they are concepts of the necessary unification of representations in a consciousness and so are principles of objectively valid judgments. This uniting in a consciousness is either analytic by identity, or synthetic by the combination and addition of various representations one to another. Experience consists in the synthetic connection of appearances (perceptions) in consciousness, so far as this connection is necessary. Hence the pure concepts of the understanding are those under which all perceptions must first be subsumed before they can serve for judgments of experience, in which the synthetic unity of the perceptions is represented as necessary and universally valid.[15]

§ 23. Judgments, when considered merely as the condition of the unification of given representations in a consciousness, are

15. But how does the proposition that judgments of experience contain necessity in the synthesis of perceptions agree with my statement so often before inculcated that experience, as cognition *a posteriori,* can afford contingent judgments only? When I say that experience teaches me something, I mean only the perception that lies in experience—for example, that heat always follows the shining of the sun on a stone; consequently, the proposition of experience is always so far contingent. That this heat necessarily follows the shining of the sun is contained indeed in the judgment of experience (by means of the concept of cause), yet is a fact not learned by experience; for, conversely, experience is first of all generated by this addition of the concept of the understanding (of cause) to perception. How perception attains this addition may be seen by referring in the *Critique* itself to the section on the transcendental faculty of judgment, B 176 *et seq.*

rules. These rules, so far as they represent the unification as necessary, are rules *a priori,* and so far as they cannot be deduced from higher rules, are principles. But in regard to the possibility of all experience, merely in relation to the form of thinking in it, no conditions of judgments of experience are higher than those which bring the phenomena, according to the different form of their intuition, under pure concepts of the understanding, and render the empirical judgments objectively valid. These are therefore the *a priori* principles of possible experience.

306

The principles of possible experience are then at the same time universal laws of nature, which can be cognized *a priori.* And thus the problem in our second question: How is pure natural science possible? is solved. For the systematization which is required for the form of a science is to be met with in perfection here, because, beyond the above-mentioned formal conditions of all judgments in general and of all rules in general, that are offered in logic, no others are possible, and these constitute a logical system. The concepts grounded thereupon, which contain the *a priori* conditions of all synthetic and necessary judgments, accordingly constitute a transcendental system. Finally, the principles by means of which all appearances are subsumed under these concepts constitute a physiological system, that is, a system of nature, which precedes all empirical cognition of nature, first makes it possible, and hence may in strictness be called the universal and pure natural science.

§ 24. The first[16] of the physiological principles[17] subsumes all appearances, as intuitions in space and time, under the concept of *quantity,* and is so far a principle of the application of mathematics to experience. The second[18] subsumes the strictly empirical element, viz., sensation, which denotes the real in intuitions, not indeed directly under the concept of *quantity,* because sensation is not an intuition that *contains* either space or time, though

16. The three following paragraphs will hardly be understood unless reference be made to what the *Critique* itself says on the subject of the principles; they will, however, be of service in giving a general view of the principles, and in fixing the attention on the main moments. [See *Critique,* B 187–294.]

17. [The Axioms of Intuition. See *Critique,* B 202–207.]

18. [The Anticipations of Perception. See *ibid.,* B 207–218.]

it puts the object corresponding to sensation in both space and time. But still there is between reality (sense-representation) and zero, or total lack of intuition in time, a difference which has a quantity. For between any given degree of light and darkness, between any degree of heat and complete cold, between any degree of weight and absolute lightness, between any degree of
307   occupied space and of totally empty space, ever smaller degrees can be thought, just as even between consciousness and total unconsciousness (psychological darkness) ever smaller degrees obtain. Hence there is no perception that can show an absolute absence; for instance, no psychological darkness that cannot be regarded as a consciousness only surpassed by a stronger consciousness. This occurs in all cases of sensation; and so the understanding can anticipate sensations, which constitute the peculiar quality of empirical representations (appearances), by means of the principle that they all have a degree, consequently, that what is real in all appearance has a degree. Here is the second application of mathematics (*mathesis intensorum*) to natural science.

§ 25. As regards the relation of appearances merely with a view to their existence, the determination is not mathematical but dynamical, and can never be objectively valid and fit for experience, if it does not come under *a priori* principles[19] by which the cognition of experience relative to appearances first becomes possible. Hence appearances must be subsumed under the concept of substance, which as a concept of the thing itself is the foundation of all determination of existence; or, secondly—so far as a succession is found among appearances, that is, an event—under the concept of an effect with reference to cause; or, lastly—so far as coexistence is to be known objectively, that is, by a judgment of experience—under the concept of community (action and reaction). Thus *a priori* principles form the basis of objectively valid, though empirical, judgments—that is, of the possibility of experience so far as it must connect objects as existing in nature. These principles are properly the laws of nature, which may be called dynamical.

Finally[20] the cognition of the agreement and connection, not

19. [The Analogies of Experience. See *ibid.*, B 218–265.]

20. [The Postulates of Empirical Thought. See *ibid.*, B 265–294.]

only of appearances among themselves in experience, but of their relation to experience in general, belongs to judgments of experience. This relation contains either their agreement with the formal conditions which the understanding cognizes, or their coherence with the material of the senses and of perception, or 308 combines both into one concept and consequently contains possibility, actuality, and necessity according to universal laws of nature. This would constitute the physiological doctrine of method (distinction between truth and hypotheses, and the bounds of the reliability of the latter).

§ 26. The third table of principles drawn from the nature of the understanding itself according to the critical method shows an inherent perfection, which raises it far above every other table which has hitherto, though in vain, been tried or may yet be tried by analyzing the objects themselves dogmatically. It exhibits all synthetic *a priori* principles completely and according to one principle, viz., the faculty of judging in general, which constitutes the essence of experience as regards the understanding, so that we can be certain that there are no more such principles. This affords a satisfaction such as can never be attained by the dogmatic method. Yet this is not all; there is a still greater merit in it.

We must carefully bear in mind the ground of proof which shows the possibility of this cognition *a priori* and, at the same time, limits all such principles to a condition which must never be lost sight of, if they are not to be misunderstood and extended in use beyond what is allowed by the original sense which the understanding places in them. This limit is that they contain nothing but the conditions of possible experience in general so far as it is subjected to laws *a priori*. Consequently, I do not say that things *in themselves* possess a quantity, that their reality possesses a degree, their existence a connection of accidents in a substance, etc. This nobody can prove, because such a synthetic connection from mere concepts, without any reference to sensuous intuition on the one side or connection of such intuition in a possible experience on the other, is absolutely impossible. The essential limitation of the concepts in these principles, then, is that all things stand necessarily *a priori* under the aforementioned conditions only *as objects of experience*.

Hence there follows, secondly, a specifically peculiar mode of

proof of these principles; they are not directly referred to ap-
309 pearances and to their relation, but to the possibility of experience, of which appearances constitute the matter only, not the
form. Thus they are referred to objectively and universally valid
synthetic propositions, in which we distinguish judgments of experience from those of perception. This takes place because appearances, as mere intuitions *occupying a part of space and time,*
come under the concept of quantity, which synthetically unites
their multiplicity *a priori* according to rules. Again, insofar as the
perception contains, besides intuition, sensation, and between
the latter and nothing (i.e., the total disappearance of sensation),
there is an ever-decreasing transition, it is apparent that the real
in appearances must have a degree, so far as it (viz., the sensation) *does not itself occupy any part of space or of time.*[21] Still the
transition to sensation from empty time or empty space is only
possible in time. Consequently, although sensation, as the
quality of empirical intuition in respect of its specific difference
from other sensations, can never be cognized *a priori,* yet it can,
in a possible experience in general, as a quantity of perception be
intensively distinguished from every other similar perception.
Hence the application of mathematics to nature, as regards the
sensuous intuition by which nature is given to us, is first made
possible and determined.

Above all, the reader must pay attention to the mode of proof
of the principles which occur under the title of Analogies of Experience. For these do not refer to the generation of intuitions,
as do the principles of applying mathematics to natural science in
310 general, but to the connection of their existence in experience;
and this can be nothing but the determination of their existence

21. Heat and light are in a small space just as large, as to degree, as in a large
one; in like manner the internal representations, pain, consciousness in general, whether they last a short or a long time, need not vary as to the degree.
Hence the quantity is here in a point and in a moment just as great as in any
space or time, however great. Degrees are thus quantities not in intuition but
in mere sensation (or the quantity of the content of an intuition). Hence they
can only be estimated quantitatively by the relation of 1 to 0, viz., by their ca-
pability of decreasing by infinite intermediate degrees to disappearance, or of
increasing from naught through infinite gradations to a determinate sensation
in a certain time. *Quantitas qualitatis est gradus* [the quantity of quality is de-
gree].

in time according to necessary laws, under which alone the connection is objectively valid and thus becomes experience. The proof, therefore, does not turn on the synthetic unity in the connection of things in themselves, but merely of perceptions, and of these, not in regard to their content, but to the determination of time and of the relation of their existence in it according to universal laws. If the empirical determination in relative time is indeed to be objectively valid (i.e., experience), these universal laws thus contain the necessity of the determination of existence in time generally (viz., according to a rule of the understanding *a priori*). Since these are prolegomena I cannot further descant on the subject, but my reader (who has probably long been accustomed to consider experience as a mere empirical synthesis of perceptions, and hence has not considered that it goes much beyond them since it imparts to empirical judgments universal validity, and for that purpose requires a pure and *a priori* unity of the understanding) is recommended to pay special attention to this distinction of experience from a mere aggregate of perceptions and to judge the mode of proof from this point of view.

§ 27. Now we are prepared to remove Hume's doubt. He justly maintains that we cannot comprehend by reason the possibility of causality, that is, of the reference of the existence of one thing to the existence of another which is necessitated by the former. I add that we comprehend just as little the concept of subsistence, that is, the necessity that at the foundation of the existence of things there lies a subject which cannot itself be a predicate of any other thing; nay, we cannot even form a concept of the possibility of such a thing (though we can point out examples of its use in experience). The very same incomprehensibility affects the community of things, as we cannot comprehend how from the state of one thing an inference to the state of quite another thing beyond it, and *vice versa,* can be drawn, and how substances which have each their own separate existence should depend upon one another necessarily. But I am very far from holding these concepts to be derived merely from experience, and the necessity represented in them to be fictitious and a mere illusion produced in us by long habit. On the contrary, I have amply shown that they and the principles derived from them are firmly established *a priori* before all expe-

311

rience and have their undoubted objective rightness, though only with regard to experience.

§ 28. Though I have no conception of such a connection of things in themselves, how they can either exist as substances, or act as causes, or stand in community with others (as parts of a real whole) and I can just as little think such properties in appearances as such (because those concepts contain nothing that lies in the appearances, but only what the understanding alone must think), we have yet a concept of such a connection of representations in our understanding and in judgments generally. This is the concept that representations belong in one sort of judgments as subject in relation to predicates; in another as ground in relation to consequent; and, in a third, as parts which constitute together a total possible cognition. Further we know *a priori* that without considering the representation of an object as determined with regard to one or the other of these moments, we can have no valid cognition of the object; and, if we should occupy ourselves with the object in itself, there is not a single possible attribute by which I could know that it is determined with regard to one or the other of these moments, that is, belonged under the concept of substance, or of cause, or (in relation to other substances) of community, for I·have no conception of the possibility of such a connection of existence. But the question is not how things in themselves but how the empirical cognition of things is determined, as regards the above moments of judgments in general, that is, how things, as objects of experience, can and must be subsumed under these concepts of the understanding. And then it is clear that I completely comprehend, not only the possibility, but also the necessity, of subsuming all appearances under these concepts, that is, of using them as principles of the possibility of experience.

312 § 29. In order to put to a test Hume's problematic concept (his *crux metaphysicorum*), the concept of cause, we have, in the first place, given *a priori* by means of logic the form of a conditional judgment in general, i.e., we have one given cognition as antecedent and another as consequent. But it is possible that in perception we may meet with a rule of relation which runs thus: that a certain appearance is constantly followed by another (though not conversely); and this is a case for me to use the

hypothetical judgment and, for instance, to say that if the sun shines long enough upon a body it grows warm. Here there is indeed as yet no necessity of connection, or concept of cause. But I proceed and say that if this proposition, which is merely a subjective connection of perceptions, is to be a judgment of experience, it must be regarded as necessary and universally valid. Such a proposition would be that the sun is by its light the cause of heat. The empirical rule is now considered as a law, and as valid not merely of appearances but valid of them for the purposes of a possible experience which requires universal and therefore necessarily valid rules. I therefore easily comprehend the concept of cause as a concept necessarily belonging to the mere form of experience, and its possibility as a synthetic unification of perceptions in a consciousness in general; but I do not at all comprehend the possibility of a thing in general as a cause, inasmuch as the concept of cause denotes a condition not at all belonging to things, but to experience. For experience can only be an objectively valid cognition of appearances and of their succession, only so far as the antecedent appearances can be conjoined with the consequent ones according to the rule of hypothetical judgments.

§ 30. Hence if the pure concepts of the understanding try to go beyond objects of experience and be referred to things in themselves *(noumena)*, they have no meaning whatever. They serve, as it were, only to spell out appearances, so that we may be able to read them as experience. The principles which arise from their reference to the sensible world only serve our understanding for use in experience. Beyond this they are arbitrary combinations without objective reality; and we can neither cognize their possibility *a priori*, nor verify their reference to objects, let alone make such reference understandable, by any example, because examples can only be borrowed from some possible experience, and consequently the objects of these concepts can be found nowhere but in a possible experience.   313

This complete (though to its originator unexpected) solution of Hume's problem rescues for the pure concepts of the understanding their *a priori* origin and for the universal laws of nature their validity as laws of the understanding, yet in such a way as to limit their use to experience, because their possibility depends solely on the reference of the understanding to experience, but with a completely reversed mode of connection which never occured to Hume: they are not derived from experience, but experience is derived from them.

This is, therefore, the result of all our foregoing inquiries: "All synthetic principles *a priori* are nothing more than principles of possible experience" and can never be referred to things in themselves, but only to appearances as objects of experience. And hence pure mathematics as well as pure natural science can never be referred to anything more than mere appearances, and can only represent either that which makes experience in general possible, or else that which, as it is derived from these principles, must always be capable of being represented in some possible experience.

§ 31. And thus we have at last something determinate upon which to depend in all metaphysical enterprises, which have hitherto, boldly enough but always at random, attempted everything without discrimination. That the goal of their exertions should be set up so close struck neither the dogmatic thinkers nor those who, confident in their supposed sound common sense, started with concepts and principles of pure reason (which were legitimate and natural, but destined for mere empirical use) in search of insights for which they neither knew nor could 314 know any determinate bounds, because they had never reflected nor were able to reflect on the nature or even on the possibility of such a pure understanding.

Many a naturalist of pure reason (by which I mean the man who believes he can decide in matters of metaphysics without any science) may pretend that he, long ago, by the prophetic spirit of his sound sense, not only suspected but knew and comprehended what is here propounded with so much ado, or, if he likes, with prolix and pedantic pomp: "that with all our reason we can never reach beyond the field of experience." But when he is questioned about his rational principles individually, he must grant that there are many of them which he has not taken from experience and which are therefore independent of it and valid *a priori*. How then and on what grounds will he restrain both himself and the dogmatist, who makes use of these concepts and principles beyond all possible experience because they are recognized to be independent of it? And even he, this adept in sound sense, in spite of all his assumed and cheaply acquired wisdom, is not exempt from wandering inadvertently beyond objects of experience into the field of chimeras. He is often deeply enough involved in them, though in announcing everything as mere probability, rational conjecture, or analogy, he gives by his popular language a color to his groundless pretensions.

§ 32. Since the oldest days of philosophy, inquirers into pure reason have thought that, besides the things of sense, or appearances *(phenomena)*, which make up the sensible world, there were certain beings of the understanding *(noumena)*, which should constitute an intelligible world. And as appearance and illusion were by those men identified (a thing which we may well excuse in an undeveloped epoch), actuality was only conceded to the beings of the understanding.

And we indeed, rightly considering objects of sense as mere appearances, confess thereby that they are based upon a thing in itself, though we know not this thing as it is in itself but only   315
know its appearances, viz., the way in which our senses are affected by this unknown something. The understanding therefore, by assuming appearances, grants also the existence of things in themselves, and thus far we may say that the representation of such things as are the basis of appearances, consequently of mere beings of the understanding, is not only admissible but unavoidable.

Our critical deduction by no means excludes things of that sort *(noumena)*, but rather limits the principles of the Aesthetic[22] in such a way that they shall not extend to all things (as everything would then be turned into mere appearance) but that they shall hold good only of objects of possible experience. Hereby, then, beings of the understanding are admitted, but with the inculcation of this rule which admits of no exception: that we neither know nor can know anything determinate whatever about these pure beings of the understanding, because our pure concepts of the understanding as well as our pure intuitions extend to

22. [The principles of sensibility (space and time). See *Critique of Pure Reason*, B 33-B 73.]

nothing but objects of possible experience, consequently to mere things of sense; and as soon as we leave this sphere, these concepts retain no meaning whatever.

§ 33. There is indeed something seductive in our pure concepts of the understanding which tempts us to a transcendent use—a use which transcends all possible experience. Not only are our concepts of substance, of power, of action, of reality, and others, quite independent of experience, containing nothing of sense appearance, and so apparently applicable to things in themselves *(noumena),* but, what strengthens this conjecture, they contain a necessity of determination in themselves, which experience never attains. The concept of cause contains a rule according to which one state follows another necessarily; but experience can only show us that one state of things often or, at most, commonly follows another, and therefore affords neither strict universality nor necessity.

Hence concepts of the understanding seem to have a deeper meaning and content than can be exhausted by their merely empirical use, and so the understanding inadvertently adds for itself to the house of experience a much more extensive wing which it fills with nothing but beings of thought, without ever observing that it has transgressed with its otherwise legitimate concepts the bounds of their use.

316

§ 34. Two important and even indispensable, though very dry, investigations therefore became indispensable in the *Critique of Pure Reason* [viz., the two chapters "The Schematism of the Pure Concepts of the Understanding" and "The Ground of the Distinction of All Objects in General into Phenomena and Noumena"]. In the former there is shown that the senses furnish, not the pure concepts of the understanding *in concreto,* but only the schema for their use, and that the object conformable to it occurs only in experience (as the product of the understanding from materials of sensibility). In the latter there is shown that, although our pure concepts of the understanding and our principles are independent of experience, and despite the apparently greater sphere of their use, still nothing whatever can be thought by them beyond the field of experience, because they can do nothing but merely determine the logical form of the judgment with regard to given intuitions. But as there is no intuition at all beyond the field of sensibility, these pure concepts, since they cannot possibly be exhibited *in concreto,* are void of all meaning; consequently all these *noumena,* together with their sum total, the intelligible world,[23] are nothing but representations of a problem, the object of which in itself is quite possible but the solution, from the nature of our understanding, totally impossible. For our understanding is not a faculty of intuition but of the connection of given intuitions in an experience. Experience must therefore contain all the objects for our concepts; but beyond it no concepts have any meaning, since no intuition can be subsumed under them.   317

§ 35. The imagination may perhaps be forgiven for occasional vagaries and for not keeping carefully within the limits of experience, since it gains life and vigor by such flights and since it is always easier to moderate its boldness than to stimulate its languor. But the understanding which ought to *think* can never be forgiven for indulging in vagaries; for we depend upon it alone for assistance to set bounds, when necessary, to the vagaries of the imagination.

But the understanding begins its aberrations very innocently and modestly. It first discerns the elementary cognitions which inhere in it prior to all experience, but yet must always have their application in experience. It gradually drops these limits; and what is there to prevent it, inasmuch as it has quite freely derived its principles from itself? And then it proceeds first to newly thought out forces in nature, then to beings outside nature—in short, to a world for whose construction the materials cannot be wanting, because fertile fiction furnishes them abundantly, and though not confirmed is yet never refuted by

23. We speak of the "intelligible world," not (as the usual expression is) "intellectual world." For cognitions are intellectual through the understanding and refer to our world of sense also; but objects, insofar as they can be represented merely by the understanding, and to which none of our sensible intuitions can refer, are termed "intelligible." But as some possible intuition must correspond to every object, we would have to think an understanding that intuits things immediately; but of such we have not the least concept, nor of *beings of the understanding* to which it should be applied.

experience. This is the reason why young thinkers are so partial to metaphysics in the truly dogmatical manner, and often sacrifice to it their time and their talents, which might be otherwise better employed.

But there is no use in trying to moderate these fruitless endeavors of pure reason by all manner of cautions as to the difficulties of solving questions so occult, by complaints of the limits of our reason, and by degrading our assertions into mere conjectures. For if their impossibility is not distinctly shown, and reason's knowledge of itself does not become a true science, in which the field of its right use is distinguished, so to say, with geometrical certainty from that of its worthless and idle use, these fruitless efforts will never be entirely abandoned.

318   § 36. *How is nature itself possible?* This question—the highest point that transcendental philosophy can ever reach, and to which, as its boundary and completion, it must proceed—properly contains two questions.

FIRST: How is nature possible in general in the *material* sense, i.e., according to intuition, as the totality of appearances; how are space, time, and that which fills both—the object of sensation—possible in general? The answer is: by means of the constitution of our sensibility, according to which it is in its special way affected by objects which are in themselves unknown to it and totally distinct from those appearances. This answer is given in the *Critique* itself in the Transcendental Aesthetic, and in these *Prolegomena* by the solution of the first main question.

SECONDLY: How is nature possible in the *formal* sense, as the totality of the rules under which all appearances must come in order to be thought as connected in an experience? The answer must be this: it is only possible by means of the constitution of our understanding, according to which all those representations of sensibility are necessarily referred to a consciousness, and by which the peculiar way in which we think (viz., by rules) and hence also experience are possible, but must be clearly distinguished from an insight into the objects in themselves. This answer is given in the *Critique* itself in the Transcendental Logic, and in these *Prolegomena* in the course of the solution of the second main question.

But how this peculiar property of our sensibility itself is possible, or that of our understanding and of the apperception which is necessarily its basis and also that of all thinking, cannot be further analyzed or answered, because it is of them that we are in need for all our answers and for all our thinking about objects.

There are many laws of nature which we can only know by means of experience; but conformity to law in the connection of appearances, i.e., nature in general, we cannot discover by any experience, because experience itself requires laws which are *a* 319 *priori* at the basis of its possibility.

The possibility of experience in general is therefore at the same time the universal law of nature, and the principles of experience are the very laws of nature. For we know nature as nothing but the totality of appearances, i.e., of representations in us; and hence we can only derive the law of their connection from the principles of their connection in us, that is, from the conditions of their necessary unification in a consciousness, which constitutes the possibility of experience.

Even the main proposition expounded throughout this section—that universal laws of nature can be cognized *a priori*—leads of itself to the proposition that the highest legislation of nature must lie in ourselves, i.e., in our understanding; and that we must not seek the universal laws of nature in nature by means of experience, but conversely must seek nature, as to its universal conformity to law, in the conditions of the possibility of experience, which lie in our sensibility and in our understanding. For how would it otherwise be possible to know *a priori* these laws, as they are not rules of analytic cognition but truly synthetic extensions of it? Such a necessary agreement of the principles of possible experience with the laws of the possibility of nature can only proceed from one of two reasons: either these laws are drawn from nature by means of experience, or conversely nature is derived from the laws of the possibility of experience in general and is quite the same as the mere universal conformity to law of the latter. The former is self-contradictory, for the universal laws of nature can and must be cognized *a priori* (that is, independent of all experience) and must be the foundation of all empirical use of the understanding; the latter alternative therefore alone remains.[24]

320   But we must distinguish the empirical laws of nature, which always presuppose particular perceptions, from the pure or universal laws of nature, which, without being based on particular perceptions, contain merely the conditions of their necessary unification in experience. With regard to the latter, nature and possible experience are quite the same, and as the conformity to law in the latter depends upon the necessary connection of appearances in experience (without which we cannot cognize any object whatever in the sensible world), consequently upon the original laws of the understanding, it seems at first strange, but is not the less certain, to say: *the understanding does not derive its laws (a priori) from, but prescribes them to, nature.*

§ 37. We shall illustrate this seemingly bold proposition by an example, which will show that laws which we discover in objects of sensuous intuition (especially when these laws are cognized as necessary) are already held by us to be such as have been placed there by the understanding, in spite of their being similar in all points to the laws of nature which we ascribe to experience.

§ 38. If we consider the properties of the circle, by which this figure at once combines into a universal rule so many arbitrary determinations of the space in it, we cannot avoid attributing a nature to this geometrical thing. Two lines, for example, which intersect each other and the circle, howsoever they may be drawn, are always divided so that the rectangle constructed with the segments of the one is equal to that constructed with the segments of the other. The question now is: Does this law lie in the circle or in the understanding? That is, does this figure, independently of the understanding, contain in itself the ground of the law; or does the understanding, having constructed according to its concepts (of the equality of the radii) the figure itself, intro-

24. Crusius alone thought of a compromise: that a spirit who can neither err nor deceive implanted these laws in us originally. But since false principles often intrude themselves, as indeed the very system of this man shows in not a few examples, we are involved in difficulties as to the use of such a principle in the absence of sure criteria to distinguish the genuine origin from the spurious, for we never can know certainly what the spirit of truth or the father of lies may have instilled into us.

duce into it this law of the chords intersecting in geometrical pro-   321
portion? When we follow the proofs of this law, we soon perceive that it can only be derived from the condition on which the
understanding founds the construction of this figure, viz., the
equality of the radii. But if we enlarge this concept to pursue
further the unity of manifold properties of geometrical figures
under common laws and consider the circle as a conic section,
which of course is subject to the same fundamental conditions of
construction as other conic sections, we shall find that all the
chords which intersect within the circle, ellipse, parabola, and
hyperbola always intersect so that the rectangles of their segments are not indeed equal but always bear a constant ratio to
one another. If we proceed still further to the fundamental
doctrines of physical astronomy, we find a physical law of reciprocal attraction extending over the whole material nature, the
rule of which is that it decreases inversely as the square of the
distance from each attracting point, just as the spherical surfaces
through which this force diffuses itself increase; and this law
seems to be necessarily inherent in the very nature of things, so
that it is usually propounded as cognizable *a priori*. Simple as the
sources of this law are, merely resting upon the relation of
spherical surfaces of different radii, its consequence is so excel-
lent with regard to the variety and regularity of its agreement
that not only are all possible orbits of the celestial bodies conic
sections, but such a relation of these orbits to each other results
that no other law of attraction than that of the inverse square of
the distance can be thought as fit for a cosmical system.

Here, accordingly, is nature resting on laws which the understanding cognizes *a priori*, and chiefly from universal principles
of the determination of space. Now I ask: do the laws of nature
lie in space, and does the understanding learn them by merely
endeavoring to find out the enormous wealth of meaning that
lies in space; or do they inhere in the understanding and in the
way in which it determines space according to the conditions of
the synthetic unity in which its concepts are all centered? Space
is something so uniform and as to all particular properties so
indeterminate that we should certainly not seek a store of laws of
nature in it. Whereas that which determines space to assume the
form of a circle, or the figures of a cone and a sphere is the un-   322

derstanding, so far as it contains the ground of the unity of their constructions. The mere universal form of intuition, called space, must therefore be the substratum of all intuitions determinable to particular objects; and in it, of course, the condition of the possibility and of the variety of these intuitions lies. But the unity of the objects is entirely determined by the understanding, and according to conditions which lie in its own nature; and thus the understanding is the origin of the universal order of nature, in that it comprehends all appearances under its own laws and thereby brings about, in an *a priori* way, experience (as to its form), by means of which whatever is to be cognized only by experience is necessarily subjected to its laws. For we are not concerned with the nature of things in themselves, which is independent of the conditions both of our sensibility and our understanding, but with nature as an object of possible experience; and in this case the understanding, because it makes experience possible, thereby insists that the sensuous world is either not an object of experience at all, or else is nature.

Appendix to Pure Natural Science

§ 39. *Of the system of the categories.* There can be nothing more desirable to a philosopher than to be able to derive the scattered multiplicity of the concepts or the principles which had occurred to him in concrete use from a principle *a priori*, and to unite everything in this way in one cognition. He formerly only believed that those things which remained after a certain abstraction, and seemed by comparison among one another to constitute a particular kind of cognitions, were completely collected; but this was only an *aggregate*. Now he knows that just so many, neither more nor less, can constitute this kind of cognition, and perceives the necessity of his division; this constitutes comprehension. And only now has he attained a *system.*

To search in our ordinary knowledge for the concepts which do not rest upon particular experience and yet occur in all knowledge from experience, of which they constitute as it were the mere form of connection, presupposes neither greater reflection

323

nor deeper insight than to detect in a language the rules of the actual use of words generally and thus to collect elements for a grammar (in fact both inquiries are very closely related), even though we are not able to give a reason why each language has just this and no other formal constitution, and still less why exactly so many, neither more nor less, of such formal determinations in general can be found in it.

Aristotle collected ten pure elementary concepts under the name of categories.[25] To these, which were also called predicaments, he found himself obliged afterwards to add five post-predicaments,[26] some of which however (*prius, simul,* and *motus*) are contained in the former; but this rhapsody must be considered (and commended) as a mere hint for future inquirers, not as a regularly worked out idea, and hence it has, in the present more advanced state of philosophy, been rejected as quite useless.

After long reflection on the pure elements of human knowledge (those which contain nothing empirical), I at last succeeded in distinguishing with certainty and in separating the pure elementary concepts of sensibility (space and time) from those of the understanding. Thus the 7th, 8th, and 9th categories had to be excluded from the old list. And the others were of no service to me because there was no principle on which the understanding could be fully mapped out and all the functions, whence its pure concepts arise, determined exhaustively and with precision.

But in order to discover such a principle, I looked about for an act of the understanding which comprises all the rest and is differentiated only by various modifications or moments, in bringing the manifold of representation under the unity of thinking in general. I found this act of the understanding to consist in judging. Here, then, the labors of the logicians were ready at hand, though not yet quite free from defects; and with this help I was enabled to exhibit a complete table of the pure functions of the understanding, which were however undetermined 324 in regard to any object. I finally referred these functions of judging to objects in general, or rather to the condition of determin-

25. 1. *Substantia.* 2. *Qualitas.* 3. *Quantitas.* 4. *Relatio.* 5. *Actio.* 6. *Passio.* 7. *Quando.* 8. *Ubi.* 9. *Situs.* 10. *Habitus.*

26. *Oppositum, Prius, Simul, Motus, Habere.*

ing judgments as objectively valid; and so there arose the pure concepts of the understanding, concerning which I could make certain that these, and this exact number only, constitute our whole cognition of things from pure understanding. I was justified in calling them by their old name of *categories*, while I reserved for myself the liberty of adding, under the title of *predicables*, a complete list of all the concepts deducible from them by combinations, whether among themselves, or with the pure form of the appearance, i.e., space or time, or with its matter, so far as it is not yet empirically determined (viz., the object of sensation in general), as soon as a system of transcendental philosophy should be completed, with the construction of which I was engaged in the *Critique of Pure Reason* itself.

Now the essential point in this system of categories, which distinguishes it from the old rhapsody (which proceeded without any principle) and for which point alone this system deserves to be considered as philosophy, consists in this: that, by means of it, the true meaning of the pure concepts of the understanding and the condition of their use could be exactly determined. For here it became obvious that they are themselves nothing but logical functions, and as such do not constitute the least concept of an object in itself, but require some sensuous intuition as a basis. These concepts, therefore, only serve to determine empirical judgments (which are otherwise undetermined and indifferent with respect to all functions of judging) as regards these functions, thereby procuring them universal validity, and by means of them, making judgments of experience in general possible.

Such an insight into the nature of the categories, which limits them at the same time to use merely in experience, never occurred either to their first author, or to any of his successors; but without this insight (which exactly depends upon their derivation or deduction), they are quite useless and only a miserable list of names, without explanation or rule for their use. Had the ancients ever conceived such a notion, doubtless the whole study of pure rational knowledge, which under the name of metaphysics has for centuries spoiled many a sound mind, would have reached us in quite another shape and would have enlightened the human understanding instead of actually exhausting it in obscure and vain subtleties and rendering it use-

325

less for true science.

This system of categories makes all treatment of every object of pure reason itself systematic, and affords a direction or clue how and through what points of inquiry any metaphysical consideration must proceed in order to be complete; for it exhausts all the moments of the understanding, under which every other concept must be brought. In like manner the table of principles has been formulated, the completeness of which we can only vouch for by the system of the categories. Even in the division of the concepts which are to go beyond the physiological application of the understanding,[27] it is still the same clue, which, as it must always be determined *a priori* by the same fixed points of the human understanding, always forms a closed circle. There is no doubt that the object of a pure concept, either of the understanding or of reason, so far as it is to be estimated philosophically and on *a priori* principles, can in this way be completely cognized. I could not therefore omit to make use of this clue with regard to one of the most abstract ontological divisions, viz., the various distinctions of the concepts of something and of nothing, and to construct accordingly[28] a regular and necessary table of their divisions.[29]

27. [Cf. *Critique of Pure Reason*, B 402 and B 442–3.]

28. [Cf. *ibid.*, B 348.]

29. On the table of the categories many neat observations may be made, for instance: (1) that the third arises from the first and the second, joined in one concept; (2) that in those of quantity and of quality there is merely a progress from unity to totality or from something to nothing (for this purpose the categories of quality must stand thus: reality, limitation, total negation), without *correlata* or *opposita*, whereas those of relation and of modality have them; (3) that, as in logic categorical judgments are the basis of all others, so the category of substance is the basis of all concepts of actual things; (4) that, as modality in a judgment is not a distinct predicate, so by the modal concepts a determination is not superadded to things, etc. Such observations are of great use. If we, besides, enumerate all the predicables, which we can find pretty completely in any good ontology (for example, Baumgarten's), and arrange them in classes under the categories, in which operation we must not neglect to add as complete a dissection of all these concepts as possible, there will then arise a merely analytic part of metaphysics, which does not contain a single synthetic proposition and might precede the second (the synthetic), and would, by its precision and completeness, be not only useful, but, in virtue of its system, be even to some extent elegant.

326   And this system, like every other true one founded on a universal principle, shows its inestimable usefulness in that it excludes all foreign concepts which might otherwise intrude among the pure concepts of the understanding, and determines the place of every cognition. Those concepts, which under the name of *concepts of reflection* have been likewise arranged in a table according to the clue of the categories, intrude into ontology without having any privilege or legitimate claim to be among the pure concepts of the understanding. The latter are concepts of connection, and thereby of the objects themselves, whereas the former are only concepts of a mere comparison of concepts already given, and therefore are of quite another nature and use. By my systematic division[30] they are saved from this confusion. But the utility of this separate table of the categories will be still more obvious when, as will soon happen, we separate the table of the transcendental concepts of reason from the concepts of the understanding. The concepts of reason being of quite another nature and origin, their table must have quite another form from that of the concepts of understanding. This so necessary separation has never yet been made in any system of metaphysics, where as a rule these ideas of reason are all mixed up with the concepts of the understanding, like children belonging to one family—a confusion that was unavoidable in the absence of a definite system of categories.

30. [See *Critique of Pure Reason*, B 316.]

How is Metaphysics in General Possible?

§ 40. Pure mathematics and pure natural science had no need for such a deduction (as has been made for both) for the sake of their own safety and certainty. For the former rests upon its own evidence, and the latter (though sprung from pure sources of the understanding) upon experience and its thorough confirmation. Pure natural science cannot altogether refuse and dispense with the testimony of experience; hence with all its certainty it can never, as philosophy, rival mathematics. Both sciences therefore stood in need of this inquiry, not for themselves, but for the sake of another science, namely, metaphysics.

Metaphysics has to do not only with concepts of nature, which always find their application in experience, but also with pure rational concepts, which never can be given in any possible experience whatsoever. Consequently, the objective reality of these concepts (viz., that they are not mere chimeras) and also the truth or falsity of metaphysical assertions cannot be discovered or confirmed by any experience. This part of metaphysics, however, is precisely what constitutes its essential end, to which the rest is only a means, and thus this science is in need of such a deduction for its own sake. The third question now proposed relates therefore. as it were, to the root and peculiarity of metaphysics, i.e., the occupation of reason merely with itself and the supposed knowledge of objects arising immediately from this brooding over its own concepts, without requiring experience or indeed being able to reach that knowledge through experience.[31]

31. If we can say that a science is actual, at least in the idea of all men, as soon as it appears that the problems which lead to it are proposed to everybody by the nature of human reason, and hence that at all times many (though faulty) endeavors are unavoidably made in its behalf; then we are bound to say that metaphysics is subjectively (and indeed necessarily) actual, and then we justly ask how is it (objectively) possible.

Without solving this question, reason will never be satisfied. The empirical use to which reason limits the pure understanding does not fully satisfy reason's own proper destination. Every

328 single experience is only a part of the whole sphere of its domain, but the absolute totality of all possible experience is itself not experience. Yet it is a necessary problem for reason, the mere representation of which requires concepts quite different from the pure concepts of the understanding, whose use is only immanent, i.e., refers to experience so far as it can be given. Whereas the concepts of reason aim at the completeness, i.e., the collective unity, of all possible experience, and thereby go beyond every given experience. Thus they become *transcendent.*

As the understanding stands in need of categories for experience, reason contains in itself the ground of ideas, by which I mean necessary concepts whose object *cannot* be given in any experience. The latter are inherent in the nature of reason, as the former are in that of the understanding. While the ideas carry with them an illusion likely to mislead, this illusion is unavoidable though it certainly can be kept from misleading us.

Since all illusion consists in holding the subjective ground of our judgments to be objective, a self-knowledge of pure reason in its transcendent (hyperbolical) use is the only safeguard against the aberrations into which reason falls when it mistakes its destination, and transcendently refers to the object in itself that which only concerns reason's own subject and its guidance in all immanent use.

§ 41. The distinction of *ideas,* i.e., of pure concepts of reason, from the categories, or pure concepts of the understanding, as cognitions of a quite different species, origin, and use is so important a point in founding a science which is to contain the system of all these *a priori* cognitions that, without this distinction,

329 metaphysics is absolutely impossible or is at best a random, bungling attempt to build a castle in the air without a knowledge of the materials or of their fitness for one purpose or another. Had the *Critique of Pure Reason* done nothing but first point out this distinction, it would thereby have contributed more to clear up our conception of, and to guide our inquiry in, the field of metaphysics than all the vain efforts which have hitherto been made to satisfy the transcendent problems of pure reason; for one never even suspected that he was in quite another field from that of the understanding, and hence that he was classing concepts of the understanding and those of reason together, as if they were of the same kind.

§ 42. All pure cognitions of the understanding have the feature that the concepts can be given in experience, and the principles can be confirmed by it; whereas the transcendent cognitions of reason cannot either, as ideas, be given in experience or, as propositions, ever be confirmed or refuted by it. Hence whatever errors may slip in unawares can only be discovered by pure reason itself—a discovery of much difficulty, because this very reason naturally becomes dialectical by means of its ideas; and this unavoidable illusion cannot be limited by any objective and dogmatic inquiries into things, but only by a subjective investigation of reason itself as a source of ideas.

§ 43. In the *Critique of Pure Reason* it was always my greatest care to endeavor, not only carefully to distinguish the several kinds of cognition, but to derive concepts belonging to each one of them from their common source. I did this in order that by knowing whence they originated, I might determine their use with safety and also have the invaluable, but never previously anticipated, advantage of knowing the completeness of my enumeration, classification, and specification of concepts *a priori,* and of knowing it according to principles. Without this, meta- 330 physics is mere rhapsody, in which no one knows whether he has enough or whether and where something is still wanting. We can indeed have this advantage only in pure philosophy, but of this philosophy it constitutes the very essence.

As I had found the origin of the categories in the four logical functions of all judgments of the understanding, it was quite natural to seek the origin of the ideas in the three functions of syllogisms. For as soon as these pure concepts of reason (the transcendental ideas) are given, they could hardly, except they be held innate, be found anywhere else than in the same activity of reason, which, so far as it regards mere form, constitutes the logical element of syllogisms; but, so far as it represents judgments of the understanding as determined with respect to one or another form *a priori,* constitutes transcendental concepts of pure reason.

The formal difference of syllogisms makes their division into categorical, hypothetical, and disjunctive necessary. The concepts of reason founded on them contain therefore, first, the idea of the complete subject (the substantial); secondly, the idea of the complete series of conditions; thirdly, the determination of all concepts in the idea of a complete complex of that which is possible.[32] The first idea is psychological, the second cosmological, the third theological; and, as all three give occasion to dialectic, yet each in its own way, the division of the whole dialectic of pure reason into its paralogism, its antinomy, and its ideal was arranged accordingly. Through this derivation we may feel assured that all the claims of pure reason are completely represented and that none can be wanting, because the faculty of reason itself, whence they all take their origin, is thereby completely surveyed.

331 § 44. In these general considerations it is also remarkable that the ideas of reason, unlike the categories, are of no service to the use of our understanding in experience, but quite dispensable, and become even an impediment to the maxims of a rational cognition of nature. Yet in another aspect still to be determined they are necessary. Whether the soul is or is not a simple substance is of no consequence to us in the explanation of its phenomena. For we cannot render the concept of a simple being understandable sensuously and concretely by any possible experience. The concept is therefore quite void as regards all hoped-for insight into the cause of appearances and cannot at all serve as a principle of the explanation of that which internal or external experience supplies. Likewise the cosmological ideas of the beginning of the world or of its eternity *(a parte ante)* cannot be of any service to us for the explanation of any event in the world

32. In disjunctive judgments we consider all possibility as divided in respect to a particular concept. By the ontological principle of the thoroughgoing determination of a thing in general, I understand the principle that either the one or the other of all possible contradictory predicates must be assigned to any object. This is at the same time the principle of all disjunctive judgments, constituting the foundation of the totality of all possibility, and in it the possibility of every object in general is considered as determined. This may serve as a brief explanation of the above proposition: that the activity of reason in disjunctive syllogisms is formally the same as that by which it fashions the idea of a totality of all reality, containing in itself the positive member of all contradictory predicates.

itself. And finally we must, according to a right maxim of the philosophy of nature, refrain from all explanation of the design of nature as being drawn from the will of a Supreme Being, because this would not be natural philosophy but an admission that we have come to the end of it. The use of these ideas, therefore, is quite different from that of those categories by which (and by the principles built upon which) experience itself first becomes possible. But our laborious analytic of the understanding would be superfluous if we had nothing else in view than the mere cognition of nature as it can be given in experience; for reason does its work, both in mathematics and in natural science, quite safely and well without any of this subtle deduction. Therefore our critique of the understanding combines with the ideas of pure reason for a purpose which lies beyond the empirical use of the understanding; but we have above declared the use of the understanding in this respect to be totally inadmissible and without any object or meaning. Yet there must be a harmony between the nature of reason and that of the understanding, and the former must contribute to the perfection of the latter and cannot possibly upset it.

The solution of this question is as follows. Pure reason does not in its ideas point to particular objects which lie beyond the 332 field of experience, but only requires completeness of the use of the understanding in the complex of experience. But this completeness can be a completeness of principles only, not of intuitions and of objects. In order, however, to represent the ideas definitely, reason conceives them after the fashion of the cognition of an object. This cognition is, as far as these rules are concerned, completely determined; but the object is only an idea invented for the purpose of bringing the cognition of the understanding as near as possible to the completeness indicated by that idea.

PREFATORY REMARK TO THE DIALECTIC OF PURE REASON

§ 45. We have above shown in §§ 33 and 34 that the purity of the categories from all admixture of sensuous determinations may mislead reason into extending their use beyond all experience to things in themselves; for though these categories themselves find no intuition which can give them meaning or sense *in concreto,* they, as mere logical functions, can represent a thing in general, but not give by themselves alone a determinate concept of anything. Such hyperbolical objects are distinguished by the appellation of *noumena,* or pure beings of the understanding (or better, beings of thought)—such as, for example, "substance," but conceived without permanence in time; or "cause," but not acting in time, etc. Here predicates that only serve to make the conformity-to-law of experience possible are applied to these concepts, and yet they are deprived of all the conditions of intuition on which alone experience is possible, and so these concepts lose all significance.

There is no danger, however, of the understanding spontaneously making an excursion so very wantonly beyond its own bounds into the field of the mere beings of thought, unless being impelled by alien laws. But when reason, which cannot be fully satisfied with any empirical use of the rules of the understanding, as being always conditioned, requires a completion of this chain of conditions, then the understanding is forced out of its sphere. And then reason partly represents objects of experience in a series so extended that no experience can grasp it, partly even (with a view to complete the series) it seeks entirely beyond experience *noumena,* to which it can attach that chain; and so, having at last escaped from the conditions of experience, reason makes its hold complete. These are then the transcendental ideas, which, (though in accord with the true but hidden ends of the natural determination of our reason) may aim, not at extravagant concepts, but at an unbounded extension of their empirical use, yet seduce the understanding by an unavoidable illusion to a transcendent use, which, though deceitful, cannot be restrained within the bounds of experience by any resolution, but only by scientific instruction and with much difficulty.

I. The Psychological Ideas[33]

§ 46. People have long since observed that in all substances the subject proper, that which remains after all the accidents (as

33. See *Critique of Pure Reason,* "The Paralogisms of Pure Reason," A 341/B 399—A 405/B 432.

predicates) are abstracted, hence the substantial itself, remains unknown, and various complaints have been made concerning these limits to our insight. But it will be well to consider that the human understanding is not to be blamed for its inability to know the substance of things, i.e., to determine it by itself, but rather for demanding to cognize it determinately as though it were a given object, it being a mere idea. Pure reason requires us to seek for every predicate of a thing its own subject, and for this subject, which is itself necessarily nothing but a predicate, its subject, and so on indefinitely (or as far as we can reach). But hence it follows that we must not hold anything at which we can arrive to be an ultimate subject, and that substance itself never can be thought by our understanding, however deep we may penetrate, even if all nature were unveiled to us. For the specific nature of our understanding consists in thinking everything discursively, i.e., by concepts, and so by mere predicates, to which, therefore, the absolute subject must always be wanting. Hence all the real properties by which we cognize bodies are mere accidents, not even excepting impenetrability, which we can only represent to ourselves as the effect of a force for which the sub-   334 ject is unknown to us.

Now we appear to have this substance in the consciousness of ourselves (in the thinking subject), and indeed in an immediate intuition; for all the predicates of an internal sense refer to the *ego,* as a subject, and I cannot conceive myself as the predicate of any other subject. Hence completeness in the reference of the given concepts as predicates to a subject—not merely an idea, but an object—that is, the *absolute subject* itself, seems to be given in experience. But this expectation is disappointed. For the ego is not a concept,[34] but only the indication of the object of the internal sense, so far as we cognize it by no further predicate. Consequently, it cannot be itself a predicate of any other thing; but just as little can it be a determinate concept of an absolute subject, but is, as in all other cases, only the reference of the

34. Were the representation of the apperception (the ego) a concept by which anything could be thought, it could be used as a predicate of other things or contain predicates in itself. But it is nothing more than the feeling of an existence without the slightest concept and is only the representation of that to which all thinking stands in relation *(relatione accidentis).*

internal phenomena to their unknown subject. Yet this idea (which serves very well as a regulative principle totally to destroy all materialistic explanations of the internal phenomena of the soul) occasions by a very natural misunderstanding a very specious argument, which infers the nature of the soul from this supposed cognition of the substance of our thinking being. This argument is specious insofar as the knowledge of this substance falls quite without the complex of experience.

§ 47. But though we may call this thinking self (the soul) substance, as being the ultimate subject of thinking which cannot be further represented as the predicate of another thing, it remains quite empty and inconsequential if permanence—the quality which renders the concept of substances in experience fruitful—cannot be proved of it.

335   But permanence can never be proved of the concept of a substance as a thing in itself, but only for the purposes of experience. This is sufficiently shown by the first Analogy of Experience,[35] and whoever will not yield to this proof may try for himself whether he can succeed in proving, from the concept of a subject which does not exist itself as the predicate of another thing, that its existence is thoroughly permanent and that it cannot either in itself or by any natural cause come into being or pass out of it. These synthetic *a priori* propositions can never be proved in themselves, but only in reference to things as objects of possible experience.

§ 48. If, therefore, from the concept of the soul as a substance we would infer its permanence, this can hold good as regards possible experience only, not of the soul as a thing in itself and beyond all possible experience. Now life is the subjective condition of all our possible experience; consequently we can only infer the permanence of the soul in life, for the death of man is the end of all the experience that concerns the soul as an object of experience, except the contrary be proved—which is the very question in hand. The permanence of the soul can therefore only be proved (and no one cares for that) during the life of man, but not, as we desire to do, after death. This is so because the concept of substance, insofar as it is to be considered as necessarily

35. Cf. *Critique* B 224–232

combined with the concept of permanence, can be so combined only according to the principles of possible experience, and therefore for the purposes of experience only.[36]

§ 49. That there is something real outside us which not only corresponds but must correspond to our external perceptions can likewise be proved to be, not a connection of things in themselves, but for the sake of experience. This means that there is something empirical, i.e., some appearance in space outside us, that admits of a satisfactory proof; for we have nothing to do with other objects than those which belong to possible experience, because objects which cannot be given us in any experience are nothing for us. Empirically outside me is that which is intuited in space; and space, together with all the appearances which it contains, belongs to the representations whose connection, according to laws of experience, proves their objective truth, just as the connection of the appearances of the internal sense proves the actuality of my soul (as an object of the internal sense). By means of external experience I am conscious of the actuality of bodies as external appearances in space, in the same manner as by means of internal experience I am conscious of the existence of my soul in time; but this soul is cognized only as an

336

---

36. It is indeed very remarkable how carelessly metaphysicians have always passed over the principle of the permanence of substances without ever attempting a proof of it; doubtless because they found themselves abandoned by all proofs as soon as they began to deal with the concept of substance. Common sense, which felt distinctly that without this presupposition no union of perceptions in experience is possible, supplied the want by a postulate. From experience itself it never could derive such a principle, partly because material objects (substances) cannot be so traced in all their alterations and dissolutions that the matter can always be found undiminished, partly because the principle contains *necessity*, which is always the sign of an *a priori* principle. People then boldly applied this postulate to the concept of soul as a *substance*, and concluded a necessary continuance of the soul after the death of man (especially as the simplicity of this substance, which is inferred from the indivisibility of consciousness, secured it from destruction by dissolution). Had they found the genuine source of this principle—a discovery which requires deeper researches than they were ever inclined to make—they would have seen that the law of the permanence of substances finds a place for the purposes of experience only, and hence can hold good of things so far as they are to be cognized and conjoined with others in experience, but never independently of all possible experience, and consequently cannot hold good of the soul after death.

object of the internal sense by appearances that constitute an internal state and of which the being in itself, which forms the basis of these appearances, is unknown. Cartesian idealism therefore does nothing but distinguish external experience from dreaming and the conformity to law (as a criterion of its truth) of the former from the irregularity and the false illusion of the latter. In both it presupposes space and time as conditions of the existence of objects, and it only inquires whether the objects of the external senses which we, when awake, put in space are as actually to be found in it as the object of the internal sense, the soul, is in time; that is, whether experience carries with it sure criteria to distinguish it from imagination. This doubt, however, may easily be disposed of, and we always do so in common life by investigating the connection of appearances in both space and time according to universal laws of experience; and we cannot doubt, when the representation of external things throughout agrees therewith, that they constitute truthful experience. Material idealism, in which appearances are considered as such only according to their connection in experience may accordingly be very easily refuted; and it is just as sure an experience that bodies exist outside us (in space) as that I myself exist according to the representation of the internal sense (in time), for the concept "outside us" only signifies existence in space. However, as the ego in the proposition "I am" means not only the object of internal intuition (in time) but the subject of consciousness, just as body means not only external intuition (in space) but the thing in itself which is the basis of this appearance, then the question whether bodies (as appearances of the external sense) exist as bodies in nature apart from my thoughts may without any hesitation be denied. But the question whether I myself as an appearance of the internal sense (the soul according to empirical psychology) exist apart from my faculty of representation in time is an exactly similar question and must likewise be answered in the negative. And in this manner everything, when it is reduced to its true meaning, is decided and certain. The formal (which I have also called transcendental) actually abolishes the material, or Cartesian, idealism. For if space be nothing but a form of my sensibility, it is as a representation in me just as actual as I myself am, and nothing but the empirical truth of the appearances in it remains for consideration. But if this is not the case, if space and the appearances in it are something existing outside us, then all the criteria of experience outside our perception can never prove the actuality of these objects outside us.

II. THE COSMOLOGICAL IDEAS[37]   338

§ 50. This product of pure reason in its transcendent use is its most remarkable phenomenon. It serves as a very powerful agent to rouse philosophy from its dogmatic slumber and to stimulate it to the arduous task of undertaking a criticism of reason itself.

I term this idea cosmological because it always takes its object only from the sensible world and does not need any other world than that whose object is given to sense; consequently, it remains in this respect in its native home, does not become transcendent, and is therefore so far not an idea; whereas to conceive the soul as a simple substance, on the contrary, means to conceive such an object (the simple) as cannot be presented to the senses. Notwithstanding, the cosmological idea extends the connection of the conditioned with its condition (whether mathematical or dynamical) so far that experience never can keep up with it. It is therefore with regard to this point always an idea, whose object never can be adequately given in any experience.

§ 51. In the first place, the use of a system of categories becomes here so obvious and unmistakable that, even if there were not several other proofs of it, this alone would sufficiently prove it indispensable in the system of pure reason. There are only four such transcendent ideas, as many as there are classes of categories; in each of which, however, they refer only to the absolute completeness of the series of the conditions for a given conditioned. In conformity with these cosmological ideas, there are only four kinds of dialectical assertions of pure reason, which, being dialectical, prove that to each of them, on equally specious principles of pure reason, a contradictory assertion stands opposed. As all the metaphysical art of the most subtle distinction cannot prevent this opposition, it compels the philos-

37. Cf. *Critique*, "The Antinomy of Pure Reason," B 432–595.

339 opher to recur to the first sources of pure reason itself. This antinomy, not arbitrarily invented but founded in the nature of
human reason, and hence unavoidable and never ceasing, contains the following four theses together with their antitheses:

1

Thesis

The world has, as to time and space, a beginning (limit).

Antithesis

The world is, as to time and space, infinite.

2

Thesis

Everything in the world is constituted out of the simple.

Antithesis

There is nothing simple, but everything is composite.

3

Thesis

There are in the world causes through freedom.

Antithesis

There is no freedom, but all is nature.

4

Thesis

In the series of world-causes there is some necessary being.

Antithesis

There is nothing necessary in the world, but in this series all is
contingent.

§ 52a. Here is the most singular phenomenon of human reason, no other instance of which can be shown in its any other
use. If we, as is commonly done, represent to ourselves the appearances of the sensible world as things in themselves, if we
assume the principles of their combination as principles universally valid of things in themselves and not merely of experience,
as is usually, nay, without our *Critique,* unavoidably done, there
arises an unexpected conflict which never can be removed in the
common dogmatic way; because the thesis, as well as the anti-

thesis, can be shown by equally clear, evident, and irresistible proofs—for I pledge myself as to the correctness of all these proofs—and reason therefore sees that it is divided against itself, a state at which the sceptic rejoices, but which must make the critical philosopher pause and feel ill at ease.

§ 52b. We may blunder in various ways in metaphysics with- **340** out any fear of being detected in falsehood. For we never can be refuted by experience if we but avoid self-contradiction, which in synthetic though purely fictitious propositions may be done whenever the concepts which we connect are mere ideas that cannot be given (as regards their whole content) in experience. For how can we make out by experience whether the world is from eternity or had a beginning, whether matter is infinitely divisible or consists of simple parts? Such concepts cannot be given in any experience, however extensive, and consequently the falsehood either of the affirmative or the negative propostion cannot be discovered by this touchstone.

The only possible way in which reason could have revealed unintentionally its secret dialectic, falsely announced as dogmatics, would be when it were made to ground an assertion upon a universally admitted principle and to deduce the exact contrary with the greatest accuracy of inference from another which is equally granted. This is actually here the case with regard to four natural ideas of reason, whence four assertions on the one side and as many counter-assertions on the other arise, each consistently following from universally acknowledged principles. Thus they reveal, by the use of these principles, the dialectical illusion of pure reason, which would otherwise forever remain concealed.

This is therefore a decisive experiment, which must necessarily expose any error lying hidden in the assumptions of reason.[38] **341**

38. I therefore would be pleased to have the critical reader to devote to this antinomy of pure reason his chief attention, because nature itself seems to have established it with a view to stagger reason in its daring pretentions and to force it to self-examination. For every proof which I have given both of the thesis and the antithesis, I pledge myself to be responsible, and thereby to show the certainty of the inevitable antinomy of reason. When the reader is brought by this curious phenomenon to fall back upon the proof of the presumption upon which it rests, he will feel himself obliged to investigate the ultimate foundation of all the cognition of pure reason with me more thoroughly.

Contradictory propositions cannot both be false, unless the concept lying at the ground of both of them is self-contradictory; for example, the propositions, "A square circle is round," and "A square circle is not round," are both false. For, as to the former, it is false that the circle is round because it is quadrangular; and it is likewise false that it is not round, i.e., angular, because it is a circle. For the logical criterion of the impossibility of a concept consists in this, that if we presuppose it, two contradictory propositions both become false; consequently, as no middle between them is conceivable, nothing at all is thought by that concept.

§ 52c. The first two antinomies, which I call mathematical because they are concerned with the addition or division of the homogeneous, are founded on such a contradictory concept; and hence I explain how it happens that both the thesis and antithesis of the two are false.

When I speak of objects in time and in space, it is not of things in themselves, of which I know nothing, but of things in appearance, i.e., of experience, as a particular way of cognizing objects which is only afforded to man. I must not say of that which I think in time or in space, that in itself, and independent of these my thoughts, it exists in space and in time, for in that case I would contradict myself, because space and time, together with the appearances in them, are nothing existing in themselves and outside of my representations, but are themselves only 342 modes of representation, and it is palpably contradictory to say that a mere mode of representation exists outside our representation. Objects of the senses therefore exist only in experience, whereas to give them a self-subsisting existence apart from experience or prior to it is merely to represent to ourselves that experience actually exists apart from experience or prior to it.

Now if I ask about the magnitude of the world, as to space and time, it is equally impossible, with regard to all my concepts, to declare it infinite or to declare it finite. For neither assertion can be contained in experience, because experience either of an infinite space or of an infinite time elapsed, or again, of the boundary of the world by an empty space or by an antecedent empty time, is impossible; these are mere ideas. This magnitude of the world, be it determined in either way, would therefore have to exist in the world itself apart from all experience. But this contradicts the concept of a world of sense, which is merely a complex of the appearances whose existence and connection occur only in our representations, i.e. , in experience; since this latter is not an object in itself but a mere mode of representation. Hence it follows that, as the concept of an absolutely existing world of sense is self-contradictory, the solution of the problem concerning its magnitude, whether attempted affirmatively or negatively, is always false.

The same holds of the second antinomy, which relates to the division of appearances. For these are mere representations; and the parts exist merely in their representation, consequently in the division (i.e., in a possible experience where they are given) and the division reaches only as far as such experience reaches. To assume that an appearance, e.g., that of a body, contains in itself before all experience all the parts which any possible experience can ever reach is to impute to a mere appearance, which can exist only in experience, an existence previous to experience. In other words, it would mean that mere representations exist before they can be found in our faculty of representation. Such an assertion is self-contradictory, as also every solution of our misunderstood problem, whether we maintain that bodies in themselves consist of an infinite number of parts or of a finite number of simple parts.

§ 53. In the first (the mathematical) class of antinomies the 343 falsehood of the presupposition consists in representing in one concept something self-contradictory as if it were compatible (i.e., an appearance as an object in itself). But as to the second (the dynamical) class of antinomies, the falsehood of the presupposition consists in representing as contradictory what is compatible. Consequently, whereas in the first case the opposed assertions were both false, in this case, on the other hand, where they are opposed to one another by mere misunderstanding, they may both be true.

Any mathematical connection necessarily presupposes homogeneity of what is connected (in the concept of magnitude), while the dynamical one by no means requires this. When we have to deal with extended magnitudes, all the parts must be homogeneous with one another and with the whole. But in the connection of cause and effect homogeneity may indeed likewise be found but is not necessary, for the concept of causality (by means of which something is posited through something else quite different from it) does not in the least require it.

If the objects of the world of sense are taken for things in themselves and the above-mentioned laws of nature for the laws of things in themselves, the contradiction would be unavoidable. So also, if the subject of freedom were, like other objects, represented as mere appearance, the contradiction would be just as unavoidable; for the same predicate would at once be affirmed and denied of the same kind of object in the same sense. But if natural necessity is referred merely to appearances and freedom merely to things in themselves, no contradiction arises if we at the same time assume or admit both kinds of causality, however difficult or impossible it may be to make the latter kind conceivable.

In appearance every effect is an event, or something that happens in time; the effect must, according to the universal law of nature, be preceded by a determination of the causality of its cause (a state of the cause) on which the effect follows according to a constant law. But this determination of the cause to causal action must likewise be something that takes place or happens; 344 the cause must have begun to act, otherwise no succession between it and the effect could be thought. Otherwise the effect, as well as the causality of the cause, would have always existed. Therefore the determination of the cause to act must also have originated among appearances and must consequently, just like its effect, be an event, which must again have its cause, and so on; hence natural necessity must be the condition according to which efficient causes are determined. Whereas if freedom is to be a property of certain causes of appearances, it must, as regards the latter as events, be a faculty of starting them spontaneously, i.e., without the causality of the cause itself needing to begin and hence needing no other ground to determine its beginning. But then the cause, as to its causality, must not stand under time-determinations of its state, i.e., it cannot be an appearance, and must be considered a thing in itself, while only its effects would be appearances.[39] If without contradiction we can think of the beings of understanding as exercising such an influence on appearances, then natural necessity will attach to all connections of cause and effect in the sensuous world, though, on the other hand, freedom can be granted to the cause which is itself not an appearance (but the foundation of appearance). Nature and freedom therefore can without contradiction be attributed to the very same thing, but in different relations—on one side as an appearance, on the other as a thing in itself.

We have in us a faculty which not only stands in connection with its subjective determining grounds that are the natural causes of its actions and is so far the faculty of a being that itself belongs to appearances, but is also related to objective grounds that are only ideas so far as they can determine this faculty; this connection is expressed by *ought*. This faculty is called *reason,* and, so far as we consider a being (man) entirely according to this objectively determinable reason, he cannot be considered as a being of sense; but, rather, this property is that of a thing in itself, and we cannot comprehend the possibility of this property—I mean how the *ought* (which might never yet have taken place) should determine its activity and could become the cause of actions whose effect is an appearance in the sensible world. Yet the causality of reason would be freedom with regard to the effects in the sensuous world, so far as we can consider *objective grounds,* which are themselves ideas, as their determinants. For

345

39. The idea of freedom occurs only in the relation of the intellectual, as cause, to the appearance, as effect. Hence we cannot attribute freedom to matter in regard to the incessant action by which it fills its space, though this action takes place from an internal principle. We can likewise find no concept of freedom suitable to purely rational beings, for instance, to God, so far as his action is immanent. For his action, though independent of external determining causes, is determined in his eternal reason, that is, in the divine *nature*. It is only, if *something is to start* by an action, and so the effect occurs in the sequence of time, or in the world of sense (e.g., the beginning of the world), that we can put the question whether the causality of the cause must in its turn have been started or whether the cause can originate an effect without its causality itself beginning. In the former case the concept of this causality is a concept of natural necessity; in the latter, that of freedom. From this the reader will see that as I explained freedom to be the faculty of starting an event spontaneously, I have exactly hit the concept which is the problem of metaphysics.

its action in that case would not depend upon subjective conditions, consequently not upon those of time, and of course not upon the law of nature which serves to determine them, because grounds of reason give the rule universally to actions, according to principles, without influence of the circumstances of either time or place.

What I adduce here is merely meant as an example to make the thing intelligible, and does not necessarily belong to our problem, which must be decided from mere concepts independently of the properties which we meet in the actual world.

Now I may say without contradiction that all the actions of rational beings, so far as they are appearances (encountered in some experience), are subject to the necessity of nature; but the same actions, as regards merely the rational subject and its faculty of acting according to mere reason, are free. For what is required for the necessity of nature? Nothing more than the determinability of every event in the world of sense according to constant laws, i.e., a reference to cause in the appearance; in this process the thing in itself at its foundation and its causality remain unknown. But, I say, the law of nature remains, whether the rational being is the cause of the effects in the sensuous world from reason, i.e., through freedom, or whether it does not determine them on grounds of reason. For if the former is the case, the action is performed according to maxims, the effect of which as appearance is always conformable to constant laws; if the latter is the case, and the action not performed on principles of reason, it is subject to the empirical laws of sensibility, and in both cases the effects are connected according to constant laws; more than this we do not require or know concerning natural necessity. But in the former case reason is the cause of these laws of nature, and therefore free; in the latter, the effects follow according to mere natural laws of sensibility, because reason does not influence it; but reason itself is not determined on that account by the sensibility (which is impossible) and is therefore free in this case too. Freedom is therefore no hindrance to natural law in appearances; neither does this law abrogate the freedom of the practical use of reason, which is connected with things in themselves as determining grounds.

Thus practical freedom, viz., the freedom in which reason

possesses causality according to objectively determining
grounds, is rescued; and yet natural necessity is not in the least
curtailed with regard to the very same effects, as appearances.
The same remarks will serve to explain what we had to say concerning transcendental freedom and its compatibility with natural necessity (in the same subject, but not taken in one and the
same reference). For, as to this, every beginning of the action of
a being from objective causes regarded as determining grounds
is always a first beginning, though the same action is in the series
of appearances only a subordinate beginning, which must be preceded by a state of the cause which determines it and is itself
determined in the same manner by another immediately preceding. Thus we are able, in rational beings, or in beings generally
so far as their causality is determined in them as things in themselves, to think of a faculty of beginning of themselves a series
of states without falling into contradiction with the laws of
nature. For the relation of the action to objective grounds of reason is not a time-relation; in this case that which determines the
causality does not precede in time the action, because such
determining grounds represent, not a reference to objects of
sense, e.g., to causes in the appearances, but to determining
causes as things in themselves, which do not stand under conditions of time. And in this way the action, with regard to the
causality of reason, can be considered as a first beginning, while
in respect to the series of appearances as a merely subordinate   347
beginning. We may therefore without contradiction consider it
in the former aspect as free, but in the latter (insofar as it is
merely appearance) as subject to natural necessity.

As to the fourth antinomy, it is solved in the same way as the
conflict of reason with itself in the third. For, provided the cause
in the appearance is distinguished from the cause *of* the appearances (so far as it can be thought as a thing in itself), both
propositions are perfectly reconcilable: the one, that there is
nowhere in the sensuous world a cause (according to similar
laws of causality) whose existence is absolutely necessary; the
other, that this world is nevertheless connected with a necessary
being as its cause (but of another kind and according to another
law). The incompatibility of these two propositions rests entirely
upon the misunderstanding of extending what is valid merely of

appearances to things in themselves and in general of mixing both in one concept.

§ 54. This, then, is the exposition, and this is the solution of the whole antinomy in which reason finds itself involved in the application of its principles to the sensible world. The former alone (the mere exposition) would be a considerable service in the cause of our knowledge of human reason, even though the solution might fail to fully satisfy the reader, who has here to combat a natural illusion which has been but recently exposed to him and which he had hitherto always regarded as true. For one result at least is unavoidable. As it is quite impossible to prevent this conflict of reason with itself—so long as the objects of the sensible world are taken for things in themselves and not for mere appearances, which they are in fact—the reader is thereby compelled to examine over again the deduction of all our *a priori* cognition and the proof which I have given of my deduction in order to come to a decision on the question. This is all I require at present; for when in this occupation he shall have thought himself deep enough into the nature of pure reason, those con-
348   cepts by which alone the solution of the conflict of reason is possible will become sufficiently familiar to him. Without this preparation I cannot expect an unreserved assent even from the most attentive reader.

III. THE THEOLOGICAL IDEA[40]

§ 55. The third transcendental idea, which affords material for the most important but, if pursued only speculatively, transcendent and thereby dialectical use of reason, is the ideal of pure reason. Reason in this case does not, as with the psychological and the cosmological ideas, start from experience and err by exaggerating its grounds in striving to attain, if possible, the absolute completeness of their series. Rather, it totally breaks with experience and from mere concepts of what constitutes the absolute completeness of a thing in general (hence by means of the idea of a most perfect primal being) proceeds to determine the possibility and therefore the actuality of all other things. And so the mere presupposition of a being which, al-

---

40. Cf. *Critique*, "The Ideal of Pure Reason," B 595–670.

though not in the series of experiences is thought for the purposes of experience and for the sake of conceiving its connection, order, and unity, i.e., the idea, is more easily distinguished from the concept of the understanding here than in the former cases. Hence we can easily expose the dialectical illusion which arises from our making the subjective conditions of our thinking objective conditions of objects themselves, and from making an hypothesis necessary for the satisfaction of our reason into a dogma. As the observations of the *Critique* on the pretensions of trancendental theology are intelligible, clear, and decisive, I have nothing more to add on the subject.

GENERAL REMARK ON THE TRANSCENDENTAL IDEAS

§ 56. The objects which are given us by experience are in many respects inconceivable, and many questions to which the law of nature leads us when carried beyond a certain point 349 (though still quite conformably to the laws of nature) admit of no answer, as, for example, the question as to why material objects attract one another? But if we entirely quit nature or, in pursuing its combinations, exceed all possible experience, and so enter the realm of mere ideas, we cannot then say that the object is inconceivable and that the nature of things proposes to us insoluble problems. For we are not then concerned with nature or with given objects at all, but with mere concepts which have their origin solely in our reason, and with mere beings of thought; and all the problems that arise from our concepts of them must be solved, because of course reason can and must give a full account of its own procedure.[41] As the psychological,

41. Herr Platner, in his *Aphorisms*, acutely says (§§ 728, 729), "If reason be a criterion, no concept which is incomprehensible to human reason can be possible. Incomprehensibility has place in what is actual only. Here incomprehensibility arises from the insufficiency of the acquired ideas." It sounds paradoxical, but is otherwise not strange to say that in nature there is much that is incomprehensible (e.g., the faculty of generation); but if we mount still higher and go even beyond nature, everything again becomes conceivable. For we then quit entirely the objects which can be given us and occupy ourselves merely about ideas, in which occupation we can easily conceive the law that reason prescribes by them to the understanding for its use in experience, because the law is reason's own product.

cosmological, and theological ideas are nothing but pure concepts of reason, which cannot be given in any experience, the questions which reason asks us about them are put to us, not by the objects, but by mere maxims of our reason for the sake of its own satisfaction. They must all be capable of satisfactory answers, which are provided by showing that they are principles which bring our use of the understanding into thorough agreement, completeness, and synthetical unity, and that they thus hold good of experience only, but of experience as a whole. Although an absolute whole of experience is impossible, the idea of a whole of cognition according to principles in general must impart to our knowledge a peculiar kind of unity, that of a system, without which it is nothing but piecework and cannot be used for the highest purpose (which is always only the system of all purposes); I do not here refer only to the practical, but also to the highest purpose of the speculative use of reason.

350

The transcendental ideas therefore express the peculiar application of reason as a principle of systematic unity in the use of the understanding. Yet if we assume this unity of the mode of cognition to pertain to the object of cognition, if we regard that which is merely *regulative* to be *constitutive,* and if we persuade ourselves that we can by means of these ideas enlarge our cognition transcendently or far beyond all possible experience, while it only serves to render experience within itself as nearly complete as possible, i.e., to limit its progress by nothing that cannot belong to experience—if we do all this, then we suffer from a mere misunderstanding in our estimate of the proper application of our reason and of its principles and suffer from a dialectic which confuses the empirical use of reason and also sets reason at variance with itself.

CONCLUSION

On The Determination of the Bounds of Pure Reason

§ 57. The clearest arguments having been adduced, it would be absurd for us to hope that we can know more of any object than belongs to the possible experience of it or lay claim to the least knowledge of how anything not assumed to be an object of possible experience is determined according to the constitution that it has in itself. For how could we determine anything in this way, since time, space, and all the concepts of the understanding, and still more all the concepts formed by empirical intuition (or perception) in the sensible world have and can have no other use than to make experience possible? And if this condition is omitted from the pure concepts of the understanding, they do not determine any object and have no meaning whatever.

But it would be, on the other hand, a still greater absurdity if we conceded no things in themselves or declared our experience 351 to be the only possible mode of knowing things, our intuition of them in space and in time to be the only possible intuition, our discursive understanding to be the archetype of every possible understanding, and to have the principles of the possibility of experience taken for universal conditions of things in themselves.

Our principles, which limit the use of reason to possible experience, might in this way become transcendent and the limits of our reason be set up as limits of the possibility of things in themselves (as Hume's *Dialogues*[42] may illustrate) if a careful critique did not guard the bounds of our reason with respect to its empirical use and set a limit to its pretensions. Scepticism originally arose from metaphysics and its lawless dialectic. At first it might, merely to favor the empirical use of reason, announce everything that transcends this use as worthless and deceitful;

42. [David Hume, *Dialogues Concerning Natural Religion* (1779)]

by, when it was noticed that the very same prin-
̲ ̲ ̲ ̲ ̲that are used in experience insensibly and apparently with
the same right led still further than experience extends, then
men began to doubt even the propositions of experience. But
here there is no danger, for common sense will doubtless always
assert its rights. A certain confusion, however, arose in science,
which cannot determine how far reason is to be trusted, and why
only so far and no further; and this confusion can only be
cleared up and all future relapses obviated by a formal determination, on principle, of the boundary of the use of our reason.

We cannot indeed, beyond all possible experience, form a definite notion of what things in themselves may be. Yet we are not
at liberty to abstain entirely from inquiring into them; for experience never satisfies reason fully but, in answering questions, refers us further and further back and leaves us dissatisfied with
regard to their complete solution. This anyone may gather from
the dialectic of pure reason, which therefore has its good subjective grounds. Having acquired, as regards the nature of our soul,
a clear conception of the subject, and having come to the conviction that its appearances cannot be explained materialistically,
who can refrain from asking what the soul really is and, if no
concept of experience suffices for the purpose, from accounting
for it by a concept of reason (that of a simple immaterial being),
though we cannot by any means prove its objective reality? Who
can satisfy himself with mere empirical knowledge in all the cosmological questions of the duration and of the magnitude of the
world, of freedom or of natural necessity, since every answer
given on principles of experience begets a fresh question, which
likewise requires its answer and thereby clearly shows the insufficiency of all physical modes of explanation to satisfy reason?
Finally, who does not see in the thoroughgoing contingency and
dependence of all his thoughts and assumptions on mere principles of experience the impossibility of stopping there? And
who does not feel himself compelled, notwithstanding all inter-
dictions against losing himself in transcendent ideas, to seek rest
and contentment, beyond all the concepts which he can vindi-
cate by experience, in the concept of a being, the possibility of
which cannot be conceived but at the same time cannot be refuted, because it relates to a mere being of the understanding

352

and without it reason must needs remain forever dissatisfied?

Bounds (in extended beings) always presuppose a space existing outside a certain definite place and inclosing it; limits do not require this, but are mere negations which affect a quantity so far as it is not absolutely complete. But our reason, as it were, sees in its surroundings a space for the cognition of things in themselves, though we can never have determinate concepts of them and are limited to appearances only.

As long as the cognition of reason is homogeneous, determinate bounds to it cannot be thought. In mathematics and natural science human reason admits of limits but not of bounds, viz., that something indeed lies outside it, at which it can never arrive, but not that it will at any point find completion in its internal progress. The enlarging of insights in mathematics and the possibility of new discoveries are infinite; and the same is the case with the discovery of new properties of nature, of new forces and laws, by continued experience and its rational unification. But limits cannot fail to be seen here; for mathematics refers to appearances only, and what cannot be an object of sensuous intuition (such as the concepts of metaphysics and of morals) lies entirely without its sphere. It can never lead to them, but neither does it require them. There is therefore a continuous progress and approach to these sciences; and there is, as it were, a point or line of contact. Natural science will never reveal to us the internal constitution of things, which, though not appearance, yet can serve as the ultimate ground for explaining appearances. Nor does that science need this for its physical explanations. Nay, even if such grounds should be offered from other sources (for instance, the influence of immaterial beings), they must be rejected and not used in the progress of its explanations. For these explanations must only be grounded upon that which as an object of sense can belong to experience, and be brought into connection with our actual perceptions according to empirical laws. 353

But metaphysics leads us towards bounds in the dialectical attempts of pure reason (not undertaken arbitrarily or wantonly, but stimulated thereto by the nature of reason itself). And the transcendental ideas, as they do not admit of evasion and yet are never capable of realization, serve to point out to us actually not only the bounds of the use of pure reason, but also the way to determine them. Such is the end and the use of this natural pre-disposition of our reason, which has brought forth metaphysics as its favorite child, whose generation, like every other in the world, is not to be ascribed to blind chance but to an original germ, wisely organized for great ends. For metaphysics, in its fundamental features, perhaps more than any other science, is placed in us by nature itself and cannot be considered the pro-duction of an arbitrary choice or a casual enlargement in the pro-gress of experience from which it is quite disparate.

Reason with all its concepts and laws of the understanding, which are adequate to it for empirical use, i.e., within the sen-sible world, finds for itself no satisfaction because ever-recurring questions deprive us of all hope of their complete solution. The transcendental ideas, which have that completion in view, are such problems of reason. But it sees clearly that the sensible world cannot contain this completion; neither, consequently, can all the concepts which serve merely for understanding the world of sense, e.g., space and time, and whatever we have adduced under the name of pure concepts of the understanding. The sensible world is nothing but a chain of appearances con-nected according to universal laws; it has therefore no subsis-tence by itself; it is not the thing in itself, and consequently must point to that which contains the basis of this appearance, to beings which cannot be cognized merely as appearances, but as things in themselves. In the cognition of them alone can reason hope to satisfy its desire for completeness in proceeding from the conditioned to its conditions.

We have above (§§ 33, 34) indicated the limits of reason with regard to all cognition of mere beings of thought. Now, since the transcendental ideas have urged us to approach them and thus have led us, as it were, to the spot where the occupied space (viz., experience) touches the void (that of which we can know nothing, viz., noumena), we can determine the bounds of pure reason. For in all bounds there is something positive (e.g., a sur-face is the boundary of corporeal space, and is therefore itself a space; a line is a space, which is the boundary of the surface, a point the boundary of the line, but yet always a place in space), whereas limits contain mere negations. The limits pointed out in those paragraphs are not enough after we have discovered that beyond them there still lies something (though we can never cognize what it is in itself). For the question now is, What is the attitude of our reason in this connection of what we know with what we do not, and never shall, know? This is an actual connection of a known thing with one quite unknown (and which will always remain so), and though what is unknown should not become the least more known—which we cannot even hope— yet the notion of this connection must be definite, and capable of being rendered distinct.

We must therefore think an immaterial being, a world of understanding, and a Supreme Being (all mere noumena), because in them only, as things in themselves, reason finds that completion and satisfaction, which it can never hope for in the derivation of appearances from their homogeneous grounds, and be- 355 cause these actually have reference to something distinct from them (and totally heterogeneous), as appearances always presuppose an object in itself and therefore suggest its existence whether we can know more of it or not.

But as we can never cognize these beings of understanding as they are in themselves, that is, determinately, yet must assume them as regards the sensible world and connect them with it by reason, we are at least able to think this connection by means of such concepts as express their relation to the world of sense. Yet if we represent to ourselves a being of the understanding by nothing but pure concepts of the understanding, we then indeed represent nothing determinate to ourselves, and consequently our concept has no significance; but if we think of it by properties borrowed from the sensible world, then it is no longer a being of understanding but is conceived as a phenomenon and belongs to the sensible world. Let us take an instance from the concept of the Supreme Being.

The deistic concept is quite a pure concept of reason, but represents only a thing containing all realities, without being able to determine any one of them; because for that purpose an example must be taken from the world of sense, in which case I should have an object of sense only, not something quite heterogeneous which can never be an object of sense. Suppose I attribute to the Supreme Being understanding, for instance; I have no concept of an understanding other than my own, one that must receive its intuitions by the senses and which is occupied in bringing them under rules of the unity of consciousness. Then the elements of my concept would always lie in the appearance; I should, however, by the insufficiency of the appearances be required to go beyond them to the concept of a being which neither depends upon appearances nor is bound up with them as conditions of its determination. But if I separate understanding from sensibility to obtain a pure understanding, then nothing remains but the mere form of thinking without intuition, by which form alone I can cognize nothing determinate and consequently no object. For that purpose I should have to think another understanding, such as would intuit its objects but of which I have not the least concept, because the human understanding is discursive, and can cognize only by means of general concepts. And the very same difficulties arise if we attribute a will to the Supreme Being; for I have this concept only by drawing it from my inner experience, and therefore from my dependence for satisfaction upon objects whose existence I require; and so the concept rests upon sensibility, which is wholly incompatible with the pure concept of the Supreme Being.

356

Hume's objections to deism are weak, and affect only the proofs, and not the deistic assertion itself. But as regards theism, which depends on a stricter determination of the concept of the Supreme Being, which in deism is merely transcendent, they are very strong and, as this concept is formed, in certain (in fact in all common) cases irrefutable. Hume always insists that by the mere concept of an original being to which we apply only ontological predicates (eternity, omnipresence, omnipotence) we think nothing determinate, and that properties which can yield a concept *in concreto* must be superadded. He insists also that it is not enough to say that it is cause, but we must explain the nature of its causality, e.g., that of an understanding and of a will. He then begins his attacks on the essential point itself, i.e., theism, as he had previously directed his battery only against the proofs of deism, an attack which is not very dangerous to it in its consequences. All his dangerous arguments refer to anthropomorphism, which he holds to be inseparable from theism and to make it contradictory in itself; but if the former can be abandoned, the latter must vanish with it and nothing remain but deism, of which nothing can come, which is of no value and which cannot serve as any foundation to religion or morals. If this anthropomorphism were really unavoidable, no proofs whatever of the existence of a Supreme Being, even were they all granted, could determine for us the concept of this Being without involving us in contradictions.

If we connect with the command to avoid all transcendent judgments of pure reason the command (which apparently conflicts with it) to proceed to concepts that lie beyond the field of its immanent (empirical) use, we discover that both can subsist together, but only at the boundary of all permitted use of reason. For this boundary belongs to the field of experience as well as to that of the beings of thought, and we are thereby taught how these remarkable ideas serve merely for marking the bounds of human reason. On the one hand, they give warning not boundlessly to extend cognition by experience, as if nothing but world remained for us to cognize, and yet, on the other hand, not to transgress the bounds of experience and to think of judging about things beyond them as things in themselves.

But we stop at this boundary if we limit our judgment merely to the relation which the world may have to a being whose very concept lies beyond all the cognition which we can attain within the world. For we then do not attribute to the Supreme Being any of the properties in themselves by which we represent objects of experience, and thereby avoid *dogmatic* anthropomorphism; but we attribute them to his relation to the world and allow ourselves a *symbolic* anthropomorphism, which in fact concerns language only and not the object itself.

If I say that we are compelled to consider the world *as if* it were the work of a Supreme Understanding and Will, I really say nothing more than that a watch, a ship, a regiment bears the same relation to the watchmaker, the shipbuilder, the commanding officer as the world of sense (or whatever constitutes the substratum of this complex of appearances) does to the unknown, which I do not hereby cognize as it is in itself but as it is for me, i.e., in relation to the world of which I am a part.

§ 58. Such a cognition is one of analogy and does not signify (as is commonly understood) an imperfect similarity of two things, but a perfect similarity of relations between two quite dissimilar things.[43] By means of this analogy, however, there remains a concept of the Supreme Being sufficiently determined *for us*, though we have left out everything that could determine it absolutely and *in itself*; for we determine it as regards the world and therefore as regards ourselves, and more do we not require. The attacks which Hume makes upon those who would determine this concept absolutely, by taking the materials for so doing from themselves and the world, do not affect us; and he cannot object to us that we have nothing left if we take away the objective anthropomorphism from our concept of the Supreme Being.

For let us assume at the outset (as Hume in his *Dialogues* makes Philo grant Cleanthes), as a necessary hypothesis, the deistic concept of the First Being, in which this Being is thought by the mere ontological predicates of substance, of cause, etc. This must be done because reason, actuated in the sensible world by mere conditions which are themselves in turn always conditioned, cannot otherwise have any satisfaction; and it therefore can be done without falling into anthropomorphism (which transfers predicates from the world of sense to a being quite distinct from the world) because those predicates are mere categories which, though they do not give a determinate concept of this being, yet give a concept not limited to any conditions of sensibility. Thus nothing can prevent our predicating of this being a causality through reason with regard to the world, and

43. Thus there is an analogy between the juridical relation of human actions and the mechanical relation of moving forces. I never can do anything to another man without giving him a right to do the same to me on the same conditions; just as no body can act with its moving force on another body without thereby causing the other to react equally against it. Here right and moving force are quite dissimilar things, but in their relation there is complete similarity. By means of such an analogy, I can obtain a relational concept of things which are absolutely unknown to me. For instance, as the promotion of the welfare of children (= a) is to the love of parents (= b), so the welfare of the human species (= c) is to that unknown in God (= x), which we call love; not as if it had the least similarity to any human inclination, but because we can posit its relation to the world to be similar to that which things of the world bear one another. But the relational concept in this case is a mere category, viz., the concept of cause, which has nothing to do with sensibility.

thus passing to theism, without being obliged to attribute to this being itself this kind of reason, as a property inhering in it. For **359** as to the former, the only possible way of pushing the use of reason (as regards all possible experience in complete harmony with itself) in the world of sense to the highest point is to assume a supreme reason as a cause of all the connections in the world. Such a principle must be quite advantageous to reason and can hurt it nowhere in its application to nature. As to the latter, reason is thereby not transferred as a property to the First Being in itself, but only to its relation to the world of sense, and so anthropomorphism is entirely avoided. For nothing is considered here but the cause of the rational form which is found everywhere in the world, and reason is attributed to the Supreme Being so far as it contains the ground of this rational form in the world, but according to analogy only, i.e., so far as this expression shows merely the relation which the Supreme Cause, unknown to us, has to the world in order to determine everything in it conformably to reason in the highest degree. We are thereby kept from using reason as an attribute in order to think God, but not kept from thinking the world in such a manner as is necessary to have the greatest possible use of reason within it according to principle. We thereby acknowledge that the Supreme Being is quite inscrutable and even unthinkable in any determinate way as to what it is in itself. We are thereby kept, on the one hand, from making a transcendent use of the concepts which we have of reason as an efficient cause (by means of the will), in order to determine the Divine Nature by properties which are only borrowed from human nature, and from losing ourselves in gross and extravagant concepts; and, on the other hand, from deluging the contemplation of the world with hyperphysical modes of explanation according to our concepts of human reason which we transfer to God, and so from losing for this contemplation its proper role, according to which it should be a rational study of mere nature and not a presumptuous derivation of its appearances from a Supreme Reason. The expression suited to our feeble concepts is that we conceive the world *as if* it came, regarding its existence and its inner determination, from a Supreme Reason. By this conception we both cognize the constitution which belongs to the world itself without pretending to determine the nature of its cause in itself, and we transfer the ground of this constitution (of the rational form of the world) to the *relation* of the Supreme Cause to the world, without finding the world sufficient by itself for that purpose.[44]

Thus the difficulties which seem to oppose theism disappear by combining with Hume's principle, "not to carry the use of reason dogmatically beyond the field of all possible experience," this other principle, which he quite overlooked, "not to consider the field of experience as one which bounds itself in the eyes of our reason." The *Critique of Pure Reason* here points out the true mean between dogmatism, which Hume combats, and skepticism, which he would substitute for it—a mean which is not like other means that we find advisable to determine for ourselves as it were mechanically (by adopting something from one side and something from the other), and by which nobody is taught a better way, but such a one as can be exactly determined on principles.

§ 59. At the beginning of this note I made use of the metaphor of a boundary in order to establish the limits of reason in regard to its suitable use. The world of sense contains merely appearances, which are not things in themselves; but the understanding must assume these latter ones, viz., noumena, because it knows the objects of experience to be mere appearances. In our reason both are comprised together, and the question is, How does reason proceed to set boundaries to the understanding as regards both these fields? Experience, which contains all that belongs to the sensible world, does not bound itself; it only proceeds in every case from the conditioned to some other equally conditioned thing. Its boundary must lie quite without it, and this is the field of the pure beings of the understanding. But this field, so far as the determination of the nature of these

44. I may say that the causality of the Supreme Cause holds the same place with regard to the world that human reason does with regard to its works of art. Here the nature of the Supreme Cause itself remains unknown to me; I only compare its effects (the order of the world), which I know, and their conformity to reason to the effects of human reason, which I also know; and hence I term the former reason, without attributing to it on that account what I understand in man by this term, or attaching to it anything else known to me as its property.

beings is concerned, is an empty space tor us; and if dogmatically determined concepts are being considered, we cannot pass beyond the field of possible experience. But as a boundary is itself something positive, which belongs to what lies within as well as to the space that lies without the given complex, it is still an actual positive cognition which reason only acquires by enlarging itself to this boundary, yet without attempting to pass it because it there finds itself in the presence of an empty space in which it can think forms of things but not things themselves. But the setting of a boundary to the field of experience by something which is otherwise unknown to reason, is still a cognition which belongs to it even at this point, and by which it is neither confined within the sensible nor strays beyond the sensible, but only limits itself, as befits the knowledge of a boundary, to the relation between what lies beyond it and what is contained within it.

Natural theology is such a concept at the boundary of human reason, being constrained to look beyond this boundary to the idea of a Supreme Being (and, for practical purposes, to that of an intelligible world also), not in order to determine anything relatively to this mere being of the understanding, which lies beyond the world of sense, but in order to guide the use of reason within the world of sense according to principles of the greatest possible (theoretical as well as practical) unity. For this purpose reason makes use of the reference of the world of sense to an independent reason as the cause of all that world's connections. Thereby reason does not merely invent a being, but, as beyond the sensible world there must be something that can be thought only by the pure understanding, reason determines that something in this particular way, though only of course according to analogy.

And thus there remains our original proposition, which is the result of the whole *Critique:* "that reason by all its *a priori* principles never teaches us anything more than objects of possible experience, and even of these nothing more than can be cognized in experience." But this limitation does not prevent reason from leading us to the objective boundary of experience, viz., to the reference to something which is not itself an object of experience but must be the highest ground of all experience. Reason

362   does not, however, teach us anything concerning the thing in itself; it only instructs us as regards its own complete and highest use in the field of possible experience. But this is all that can be reasonably desired in the present case, and with it we have cause to be satisfied.

§ 60. Thus we have fully exhibited metaphysics according to its subjective possibility, as it is actually given in the natural predisposition of human reason and in that which constitutes the essential end of its pursuit. We have found that this merely natural use of such a predisposition of our reason, if no discipline arising only from a scientific critique bridles and sets limits to it, involves us in transcendent dialectical inferences, that are in part merely illusory and in part even self-contradictory, and that this fallacious metaphysics is not only unnecessary as regards the promotion of our knowledge of nature but even disadvantageous to it. There yet remains a problem worthy of inquiry, which is to find out the natural ends intended by this disposition to transcendent concepts in our reason, because everything that lies in nature must be originally intended for some useful purpose.

Such an inquiry is of a doubtful nature, and I acknowledge that what I can say about it is conjecture only, like every speculation about the first ends of nature. This conjecture may be allowed to me in this case alone, because the question does not concern the objective validity of metaphysical judgments but our natural predisposition to them, and therefore does not belong to the system of metaphysics but to anthropology.

When I compare all the transcendental ideas, the totality of which constitutes the particular problem of natural pure reason, compelling it to quit the mere contemplation of nature, to transcend all possible experience, and in this endeavor to produce the thing (be it knowledge or fiction) called metaphysics; I think I perceive that the aim of this natural tendency is to free our concepts from the fetters of experience and from the limits of the mere contemplation of nature so far as at least to open to us a field containing mere objects for the pure understanding which no sensibility can reach, not indeed for the purpose of speculatively occupying ourselves with them (for there we can

363   find no ground to stand on), but in order that practical principles might find some such scope for their necessary expectation and

hope and might expand to the universality which reason unavoidably requires from a moral point of view.

So I find that the psychological idea (however little it may reveal to me the nature of the human soul, which is elevated above all concepts of experience) shows the insufficiency of these concepts plainly enough and thereby deters me from materialism, a psychological concept which is unfit for any explanation of nature and which in addition confines reason in practical respects. The cosmological ideas, by the obvious insufficiency of all possible cognition of nature to satisfy reason in its legitimate inquiry, serve in the same manner to keep us from naturalism, which asserts nature to be sufficient for itself. Finally, all natural necessity in the sensible world is conditional, as it always presupposes the dependence of things upon others, and unconditional necessity must be sought only in the unity of a cause different from the world of sense. But as the causality of this cause, in its turn, were it merely nature, could never render the existence of the contingent (as its consequent) comprehensible, reason frees itself by means of the theological idea from fatalism (both as a blind natural necessity in the coherence of nature itself, without a first principle, and as a blind causality of this principle itself) and leads to the concept of a cause possessing freedom and hence of a Supreme Intelligence. Thus the transcendental ideas serve, if not to instruct us positively, at least to destroy the impudent and restrictive assertions of materialism, of naturalism, and of fatalism, and thus to afford scope for the moral ideas beyond the field of speculation. These considerations, I should think, explain in some measure the natural predisposition of which I spoke.

The practical value which a merely speculative science may have lies outside the bounds of this science, and can therefore be considered as a scholium merely, and like all scholia does not form part of the science itself. This application, however, surely lies within the bounds of philosophy, especially of philosophy drawn from the pure sources of reason, where its speculative use in metaphysics must necessarily be at one with its practical use in morals. Hence the unavoidable dialectic of pure reason, con- **364** sidered in metaphysics as a natural tendency, deserves to be explained not as a mere illusion, which is to be removed, but also, if possible, as a natural provision as regards its end, though this task, a work of supererogation, cannot justly be assigned to metaphysics proper.

The solutions of these questions which are treated in the *Critique*[45] should be considered a second scholium, which, however, has a greater affinity with the subject of metaphysics. For there certain rational principles are expounded which determine *a priori* the order of nature or rather of the understanding, which seeks nature's laws through experience. They seem to be constitutive and legislative with regard to experience, though they spring from mere reason, which cannot be considered, like the understanding, as a principle of possible experience. Now whether or not this harmony rests upon the fact that, just as nature does not inhere in appearances or in their source (the sensibility) itself, but only in the relation of the latter to the understanding, so also a thoroughgoing unity in the use of the understanding to bring about an entirety of all possible experience (in a system) can only belong to the understanding when in relation to reason, with the result that experience is in this way mediately subordinate to the legislation of reason: this question may be discussed by those who desire to trace the nature of reason even beyond its use in metaphysics into the general principles for making systematic a history of nature in general. I have presented this task as important, but not attempted its solution in the book itself.[46]

365   And thus I conclude the analytical solution of the main question which I had proposed: "How is metaphysics in general possible?" by ascending from the data of its actual use, at least in its consequences, to the grounds of its possibility.

45. *Critique of Pure Reason,* "The Regulative Employment of the Ideas of Pure Reason," B 670–696

46. Throughout in the *Critique* I never lost sight of the plan not to neglect anything, were it ever so recondite, that could render the inquiry into the nature of pure reason ccmplete. Everybody may afterwards carry his researches as far as he pleases, when he has been merely shown what yet remains to be done. This can reasonably be expected of him who has made it his business to survey the whole field, in order to consign it to others for future cultivation and allotment. And to this branch both the scholia belong, which will hardly recommend themselves by their dryness to amateurs, and hence are added here for connoisseurs only.

SOLUTION OF THE GENERAL QUESTION
OF THE PROLEGOMENA

"How is Metaphysics Possible as Science?"

Metaphysics, as a natural disposition of reason, is actual; but if considered by itself alone (as the analytical solution of the third principal question showed), it is dialectical and illusory. If we think of taking principles from it, and in using them follow the natural, but on that account not less false, illusion, we can never produce science, but only a vain dialectical art, in which one school may outdo another but none can ever acquire a just and lasting approbation.

In order that as a science metaphysics may be entitled to claim, not mere fallacious plausibility, but insight and conviction, a critique of reason must itself exhibit the whole stock of *a priori* concepts, their division according to their various sources (sensibility, understanding, and reason), together with a complete table of them, the analysis of all these concepts, with all their consequences and especially the possibility of synthetic cognition *a priori* by means of the deduction of these concepts, the principles and bounds of their use, all in a complete system. Critique, therefore, and critique alone contains in itself the whole well-proved and well-tested plan, and even all the means required to establish metaphysics as a science; by other ways and means it is impossible. The question here, therefore, is not so much how this performance is possible as how to set it going and induce men of clear heads to quit their hitherto perverted and fruitless cultivation for one that will not deceive, and how such a union for the common end may best be directed.

This much is certain: whoever has once tasted critique will be ever after disgusted with all dogmatical twaddle which he formerly put up with because his reason had to have something and could find nothing better for its support. Critique stands in the same relation to the common metaphysics of the schools as

366

chemistry does to alchemy, or as astronomy to the astrology of the fortune teller. I pledge myself that nobody who has thought through and grasped the principles of critique, even only in these *Prolegomena,* will ever return to that old and sophistical pseudo-science; but he will, rather, with a certain delight look forward to a metaphysics which is now indeed in his power, requiring no more preparatory discoveries, and now at last affording permanent satisfaction to reason. For here is an advantage upon which, of all possible sciences, metaphysics alone can with certainty reckon: that it can be brought to such completion and fixity as to require no further change or be capable of any augmentation by new discoveries, because here reason has the sources of its knowledge in itself, not in objects and their observation, by which its stock of knowledge could be further increased. When, therefore, it has exhibited the fundamental laws of its faculty completely and so determinately as to avoid all misunderstanding, there remains nothing more for pure reason to cognize *a priori;* nay, there is even no ground to raise further questions. The sure prospect of knowledge so determinate and so compact has a peculiar charm, even though we should set aside all its advantages, of which I shall hereafter speak.

All false art, all vain wisdom, lasts its time but finally destroys itself, and its highest culture is also the epoch of its decay. That this time is come for metaphysics appears from the state into which it has fallen among all learned nations, despite all the zeal with which other sciences of every kind are pursued. The old arrangement of our university studies still preserves its shadow; now and then an academy of science tempts men by offering prizes to write essays on it, but it is no longer numbered among sound sciences; and let anyone judge for himself how a sophisticated man, if he were called a great metaphysician, would receive the compliment, which may be well meant but is scarcely envied by anybody.

367   Yet, though the period of the downfall of all dogmatic metaphysics has undoubtedly arrived, we are yet far from being able to say that the period of its regeneration is come by means of a thorough and complete critique of reason. All transitions from an inclination to its contrary pass through the stage of indifference, and this moment is the most dangerous for an

author but, in my opinion, the most favorable for the science. For when party spirit has died out by a total dissolution of former connections, minds are in the best state to listen to several proposals for an organization according to a new plan.

When I say that I hope these *Prolegomena* will excite investigation in the field of critique and afford a new and promising object to sustain the general spirit of philosophy, which seems on its speculative side to want sustenance, I can imagine beforehand that everyone whom the thorny paths of my *Critique* have tired and put out of humor will ask me upon what I found this hope. My answer is: upon the irresistible law of necessity.

That the human spirit will ever give up metaphysical researches is as little to be expected as that we should prefer to give up breathing altogether, in order to avoid inhaling impure air. There will, therefore, always be metaphysics in the world; nay, everyone, especially every reflective man, will have it and, for want of a recognized standard, will shape it for himself after his own pattern. What has hitherto been called metaphysics cannot satisfy any critical mind, but to forego it entirely is impossible; therefore a critique of pure reason itself must now be attempted or, if one exists, investigated and brought to the full test, because there is no other means of supplying this pressing want which is something more than mere thirst for knowledge.

Ever since I have come to know critique, whenever I finish reading a book of metaphysical contents which, by the determination of its concepts, by variety, order, and an easy style, was not only entertaining but also helpful, I cannot help asking, 368 "Has this author indeed advanced metaphysics a single step?" The learned men whose works have been useful to me in other respects and always contributed to the culture of my mental powers will, I hope, forgive me for saying that I have never been able to find either their essays or my own less important ones (though self-love may recommend them to me) to have advanced the science of metaphysics in the least, and why? Here is the very obvious reason: metaphysics did not then exist as a science, nor can it be gathered piecemeal; but its germ must be fully preformed in critique. But in order to prevent all misconception, we must remember what has already been said—that by the analytic treatment of our concepts the understanding gains indeed a great deal, but the science (of metaphysics) is thereby not in the least advanced because these analyses of concepts are nothing but the materials from which the intention is to carpenter our science. Let the concepts of substance and of accident be ever so well analyzed and determined; all this is very well as a preparation for some future use. But if we cannot prove that in all which exists the substance endures and only the accidents vary, our science is not the least advanced by all our analyses. Metaphysics has hitherto never been able to prove *a priori* either this proposition or that of sufficient reason, still less any more complex theorem such as belongs to psychology or cosmology, or indeed any synthetic proposition. By all its analyzing, therefore, nothing is affected, nothing obtained or forwarded; and the science, after all this bustle and noise, still remains as it was in the days of Aristotle, though far better preparations were made for it than of old if only the clue to synthetic cognitions had been discovered.

If anyone thinks himself offended, he is at liberty to refute my charge by producing a single synthetic proposition belonging to metaphysics which he would prove dogmatically *a priori;* for until he has actually performed this feat, I shall not grant that he has truly advanced the science, even though this proposition should be sufficiently confirmed by common experience. No demand can be more moderate or more equitable and, in the (inevitably certain) event of its nonperformance, no assertion more just than that hitherto metaphysics has never existed as a science.

369

But there are two things which, in case the challenge be accepted, I must deprecate: first, trifling about probability and conjecture, which are suited as little to metaphysics as to geometry; and secondly, a decision by means of the magic wand of socalled sound common sense, which does not convince everyone but accommodates itself to personal peculiarities.

For as to the former, nothing can be more absurd than in metaphysics, a philosophy from pure reason, to try to ground our judgments upon probability and conjecture. Everything that is to be cognized *a priori* is thereby announced as apodeictically certain, and must therefore be proved in this way. We might as well try to ground geometry or arithmetic upon conjectures. As to the calculus of probabilities in the latter, it does not contain probable but perfectly certain judgments concerning the degree of the possibility of certain cases under given uniform conditions, which, in the sum of all possible cases, must infallibly happen according to the rule, though it is not sufficiently determined as regards every single instance. Conjectures (by means of induction and analogy) can be suffered in an empirical natural science only, yet even there at least the possibility of what we assume must be quite certain.

The appeal to common sense is even more absurd, when concepts and principles are said to be valid, not insofar as they hold with regard to experience, but outside the conditions of experience. For what is common sense? It is normal good sense, so far as it judges rightly. What is normal good sense? It is the faculty of the knowledge and use of rules *in concreto,* as distinguished from the speculative understanding, which is a faculty of know ing rules *in abstracto.* Common sense can hardly understand the rule that every event is determined by means of its cause and can never comprehend it thus generally. It therefore demands an example from experience; and when it hears that this rule means nothing but what it always thought when a pane was broken or a kitchen-utensil missing, it then understands the principle and grants it. Common sense, therefore, is only of use so far as it can see its rules (though they actually are *a priori*) confirmed by experience; consequently, to comprehend them *a priori,* or independently of experience, belongs to the speculative understanding and lies quite beyond the horizon of common sense. But the province of metaphysics is entirely confined to the latter kind of knowledge, and it is certainly a bad sign of common sense to appeal to it as a witness, for it cannot here form any opinion whatever, and men look down upon it with contempt until they are in trouble and can find in their speculation neither advice nor help.

370

It is a common subterfuge of those false friends of common sense (who occasionally prize it highly, but usually despise it) to say that there must surely be at all events some propositions which are immediately certain and of which there is no occasion to give any proof, or even any account at all, because we otherwise could never stop inquiring into the grounds of our judgments. But if we except the principle of contradiction, which is not sufficient to show the truth of synthetic judgments, they can never adduce, in proof of this privilege, anything else indubitable which they can immediately ascribe to common sense, except mathematical propositions, such as twice two make four, between two points there is but one straight line, etc. But these judgments are radically different from those of metaphysics. For in mathematics I can by thinking construct whatever I represent to myself as possible by a concept: I add to the first two the other two, one by one, and myself make the number four, or I draw in thought from one point to another all manner of lines, equal as well as unequal; yet I can draw one only which is like itself in all its parts. But I cannot, by all my power of thinking, extract from the concept of a thing the concept of something else whose existence is necessarily connected with the former, but I must call upon experience. And though my understanding furnishes me *a priori* (yet only in reference to possible experience) with the concept of such a connection (i.e., causation), I cannot exhibit it *a priori* in intuition, like the concepts of mathematics, and so show its possibility *a priori.* This concept, together with the principles of its application, always requires, if it is to hold *a priori*—as is requisite in metaphysics—a justification and deduction of its possibility, because we cannot otherwise know how far it holds good and whether it can be used in experience only or beyond it also. Therefore in metaphysics, as a speculative science of pure reason, we can never appeal to common sense, but may do so only when (in certain matters) we are forced to surrender it and renounce all pure speculative cognition, which must always be theoretic knowledge, and therefore are forced to forego metaphysics itself and its instruction for the sake of adopting a rational faith which alone may be possible for us, sufficient to our wants, and perhaps even more salutary than knowledge itself. For then the shape of the thing is quite altered. Metaphysics must be science, not only as a whole but in all its parts; otherwise it is nothing at all, because as speculation of pure reason it finds a hold only on universal insights. Beyond its field, however, probability and common sense may be used advantageously and justly, but on quite special principles, the importance of which always depends on their reference to the practical.

This is what I hold myself justified in requiring for the possibility of metaphysics as a science.

APPENDIX

On What Can Be Done to Make Metaphysics
As a Science Actual

Since all the ways heretofore taken have failed to attain the goal, and since without a preceding critique of pure reason it is not likely ever to be attained, the attempt before us has a right to an accurate and careful examination, unless it be thought more advisable to give up all pretensions to metaphysics, to which, if **372** men would but consistently adhere to their purpose, no objection can be made. If we take the course of things as it is, not as it ought to be, there are two sorts of judgments: (1) one a judgment which precedes investigation (in our case one in which the reader from his own metaphysics pronounces judgment on the *Critique of Pure Reason,* which was intended to discuss the very possibility of metaphysics); (2) the other a judgment subsequent to investigation. In the latter, the reader is enabled to ignore for a while the consequences of the critical researches that may be repugnant to his formerly adopted metaphysics, and first examines the grounds whence those consequences are derived. If what common metaphysics propounds were demonstrably certain (like geometry) the former way of judging would hold good. For if the consequences of certain principles are repugnant to established truths, these principles are false and without further inquiry to be repudiated. But if metaphysics does not possess a stock of indisputably certain (synthetic) propositions, and should it even be the case that there are a number of them, which, though among the most plausible, are by their consequences in mutual conflict, and if no sure criterion of the truth of peculiarly metaphysical (synthetic) propositions is to be met with in it, then the former way of judging is not admissible, but the investigation of the principles of the *Critique* must precede all judgments as to its value.

111

A Specimen of a Judgment about the Critique
Prior to Its Examination.

Such a judgment is to be found in the *Göttingische gelehrte Anzeigen,* in the supplement to the third part, of January 19, 1782, pages 40 *et seq.*[47]

When an author who is familiar with the subject of his work and endeavors to present his independent reflections in its elaboration falls into the hands of a reviewer who, in his turn, is keen enough to discern the points on which the worth or worthlessness of the books rests, who does not cling to words but goes to the heart of the subject, sifting and testing the principles which the author takes as his point of departure, the severity of the judgment may indeed displease the author, but the public does not care, as it gains thereby. And the author himself may be satisfied at having an opportunity of correcting or explaining his positions at an early date by the examination of a competent judge, in such a manner that if he believes himself fundamentally right, he can remove in time any stumbling-block that might hurt the success of his work.

I find myself, with my reviewer, in quite another position. He seems not to see at all the real matter of the investigation, with which (successfully or unsuccessfully) I have been occupied. It is either impatience at thinking out a lengthy work, or vexation at a threatened reform of a science in which he believed he had brought everything to perfection long ago, or, what I am reluctant to suppose, real narrow-mindedness that prevents him from ever carrying his thoughts beyond his school metaphysics. In short, he passes impatiently in review a long series of propositions, of which, without knowing their premises, one can comprehend nothing, intersperses here and there his censure, the reason of which the reader understands just as little as the propositions against which it is directed; and hence [his report] can neither serve the public nor damage me in the judgment of experts. I should, for these reasons, have passed over this judgment altogether, were it not that it may afford me occasion for

373

47. [This review was given by Christian Garve.]

some explanations which may in some cases save the readers of these *Prolegomena* from a misconception.

In order to take a position from which my reviewer could most easily set the whole work in a most unfavorable light, without venturing to trouble himself with any special investigation, he begins and ends by saying: "This work is a system of transcendental (or, as he translates it, of higher[48]) idealism."

A glance at this line soon showed me the sort of criticism that **374** I had to expect, much as though the reviewer were one who had never seen or heard of geometry, having found a Euclid and coming upon various figures in turning over its leaves, were to say, on being asked his opinion of it: "The work is a textbook of drawing; the author introduces a peculiar terminology in order to give dark, incomprehensible directions, which in the end teach nothing more than what everyone can effect by a fair natural accuracy of eye, etc."

Let us see, in the meantime, what sort of an idealism it is that goes through my whole work, although it does not by a long way constitute the soul of the system.

The dictum of all genuine idealists, from the Eleatic school to Bishop Berkeley, is contained in this formula: "All cognition through the senses and experience is nothing but sheer illusion, and only in the ideas of the pure understanding and reason is there truth."

The principle that throughout dominates and determines my idealism is, on the contrary: "All cognition of things merely from pure understanding or pure reason is nothing but sheer illusion, and only in experience is there truth."

---

48. By no means "higher." High towers and metaphysically great men resembling them, round both of which there is commonly much wind, are not for me. My place is the fruitful bathos of experience; and the word "transcendental," the meaning of which is so often indicated by me but not once grasped by my reviewer (so carelessly has he regarded everything), does not signify something passing beyond all experience but something that indeed precedes it *a priori*, but that is intended simply to make cognition of experience possible. If these concepts overstep experience, their use is termed "transcendent," which must be distinguished from the immanent use, i.e., use restricted to experience. All misunderstandings of this kind have been sufficiently guarded against in the work itself, but my reviewer found his advantage in misunderstanding me.

But this is directly contrary to idealism proper. How came I then to use this expression for quite an opposite purpose, and how came my reviewer to see it everywhere? The solution of this difficulty rests on something that could have been very easily understood from the context of the work, if the reader had only desired to do so. Space and time, together with all that they contain, are not things in themselves or their qualities but belong merely to the appearances of the things in themselves; up to this point I am one in confession with the above idealists. But these, and among them more particularly Berkeley, regarded space as a mere empirical representation that, like the appearances it contains, is, together with its deter-
375 minations, known to us only by means of experience or perception. I, on the contrary, prove in the first place that space (and also time, which Berkeley did not consider) and all its determinations can be cognized *a priori* by us, because, no less than time, it inheres in us as a pure form of our sensibility before all perception of experience and makes possible all intuition of sensibility, and therefore all appearances. It follows from this that, as truth rests on universal and necessary laws as its criteria, experience, according to Berkeley, can have no criteria of truth because its appearances (according to him) have nothing *a priori* at their foundation, whence it follows that experience is nothing but sheer illusion; whereas with us, space and time (in conjunction with the pure concepts of the understanding) prescribe their law *a priori* to all possible experience and, at the same time, afford the certain criterion for distinguishing truth from illusion therein.[49]

My so-called (properly critical) idealism is of quite a special kind, in that it reverses the usual idealism and through my kind all *a priori* cognition, even that of geometry, first receives objective reality, which, without my demonstrated ideality of space and time, could not be maintained by the most zealous realists.

49. Idealism proper always has a mystical tendency, and can have no other; but mine is solely designed for the purpose of comprehending the possibility of our *a priori* cognition of objects of experience, which is a problem never hitherto solved or even suggested. In this way all mystical idealism falls to the ground, for (as may be seen in Plato) it inferred from our cognitions *a priori* (even from those of geometry) another intuition different from that of the senses (namely, an intellectual intuition), because it never occurred to anyone that the senses themselves might intuit *a priori*.

This being the state of the case, I could wish, in order to avoid all misunderstanding, to have named this concept of mine otherwise, but to alter it altogether is probably impossible. It may therefore be permitted me in future, as has been above intimated, to term it "formal" or, better still, "critical" idealism, to distinguish it from the dogmatic idealism of Berkeley and from the skeptical idealism of Descartes.

Beyond this, I find nothing remarkable in the judgment of my book. The reviewer makes sweeping criticisms, a mode prudently chosen, since it does not betray one's own knowledge or ignorance; a single thorough criticism in detail, had it touched the main question, as is only fair, would have exposed either my error or my reviewer's measure of insight into this kind of inquiry. It was, moreover, not a badly conceived plan, in order at once to take from readers (who are accustomed to form their conceptions of books from newspaper reports) the desire to read the book itself, to pour out one after the other in one breath a number of propositions which, torn from their connection with their premises and explanations, must necessarily sound senseless, especially considering how antipathetic they are to all school-metaphysics; to exhaust the reader's patience *ad nauseam,* and then, having made me acquainted with the lucid propostion that persistent illusion is truth, to conclude with the crude paternal moralization: to what end, then, the quarrel with accepted language; to what end, and whence, the idealistic distinction? A judgment which seeks all that is characteristic of my book, first supposed to be metaphysically heterodox, in a mere innovation of the nomenclature proves clearly that my would-be judge has understood nothing of the subject and, in addition, has not understood himself.[50]

376

50. The reviewer often fights with his own shadow. When I oppose the truth of experience to dream, he never thinks that I am here speaking simply of the well-known *somnio objective sumto* ["dreams taken objectively"—Christian Wolff's *German Metaphysics,* § 142] of the Wolffian philosophy, which is merely formal, and with which the distinction between sleeping and waking is in no way concerned—a distinction which can indeed have no place in a transcendental philosophy. For the rest, he calls my deduction of the categories and table of the principles of the understanding "common well-known axioms of logic and ontology, expressed in an idealistic manner." The reader need only consult these *Prolegomena* upon this point to convince himself that a more miserable and historically incorrect judgment could hardly be made.

My reviewer speaks like a man who is conscious of important and superior insight which he keeps hidden, for I am aware of nothing recent with respect to metaphysics that could justify his tone. But he is quite wrong to withhold his discoveries from the world, for there are doubtless many who, like myself, have not been able to find in all the fine things that have for long past been written in this department anything that has advanced the science by so much as a finger's breadth. We find indeed the giving a new point to definitions, the supplying of lame proofs with new crutches, the adding to the crazy-quilt of metaphysics fresh patches or changing its pattern; but all this is not what the world requires. The world is tired of metaphysical assertions; what is wanted is the possibility of this science, the sources from which certainty therein can be derived, and certain criteria by which it may distinguish the dialectical illusion of pure reason from truth. To this the critic seems to possess a key, otherwise he would never have spoken out in such a high tone.

377

But I am inclined to suspect that no such requirement of the science has ever entered his thoughts, for in that case he would have directed his judgment to this point, and even a mistaken attempt in such an important matter would have won his respect. If that be the case, we are once more good friends. He may penetrate as deeply as he likes into his metaphysics, without any one hindering him; only as concerns that which lies outside metaphysics, its sources, which are to be found in reason, he cannot form a judgment. That my suspicion is not without foundation is proved by the fact that he does not mention a word about the possibility of synthetic knowledge *a priori,* the special problem upon the solution of which the fate of metaphysics wholly rests and upon which my *Critique* (as well as the present *Prolegomena)* entirely hinges. The idealism he encountered and which he hung upon was only taken up in the doctrine as the sole means of solving the above problem (although it received its confirmation on other grounds), and hence he must have shown either that the above problem does not possess the importance I attribute to it (even in these *Prolegomena*) or that, by my concept of appearances, it is either not solved at all or can be better solved in another way; but I do not find a word of this in the criticism. The reviewer, then, understands nothing of my work and possibly also nothing of the spirit and essential nature of metaphysics itself; and it is not, what I would rather assume, the haste of a reviewer to finish his review, incensed at the labor of plodding through so many obstacles, that threw an unfavorable shadow over the work lying before him and made its fundamental features unrecognizable.

There is a great deal to be done before a learned journal, it 378 matters not with what care its writers may be selected, can maintain its otherwise well-merited reputation in the field of metaphysics as elsewhere. Other sciences and branches of knowledge have their standard. Mathematics has it in itself, history and theology in secular or sacred books, natural science and the art of medicine in mathematics and experience, jurisprudence in law books, and even matters of taste in the examples of the ancients. But for the judgment of the thing called metaphysics, the standard has yet to be found. I have made an attempt to determine it, as well as its use. What is to be done, then, until it be found, when works of this kind have to be judged? If they are of a dogmatic character, one may do what one likes; no one will play the master over others here for long before someone else appears to deal with him in the same manner. If, however, they are critical in character, not indeed with reference to other works but to reason itself, so that the standard of judgment cannot be assumed but has first of all to be sought for, then, though objection and blame may indeed be permitted, yet a certain degree of leniency is indispensable, since the need is common to us all and the lack of the necessary insight makes the high-handed attitude of judge unwarranted.

In order, however, to connect my defense with the interest of the philosophical commonwealth, I propose a test, which must be decisive as to the mode whereby all metaphysical investigations may be directed to their common purpose. This is nothing more that what mathematicians have done in establishing the advantage of their methods by competition. I challenge my critic to demonstrate, as is only just, on *a priori* grounds, in his own way, any single really metaphysical principle asserted by him. Being metaphysical, it must be synthetic and cognized *a priori* from concepts, but it may also be any one of the most indispensable propositions, as, for instance, the principle of the permanence of substance or of the necessary determination of events in the world by their causes. If he cannot do this (silence however is confession), he must admit that, since metaphysics without apodeictic certainty of propositions of this kind is nothing at all, its possibility or impossibility must before all things be **379** established in a critique of pure reason. Thus he is bound either to confess that my principles in the *Critique* are correct, or he must prove their invalidity. But as I can already foresee that, confidently as he has hitherto relied on the certainty of his principles, when it comes to a strict test he will not find a single one in the whole range of metaphysics he can boldly bring forward, I will concede to him an advantageous condition, which can only be expected in such a competition, and will relieve him of the *onus probandi* by laying it on myself.

He finds in these *Prolegomena* and in my *Critique*[51] eight propositions, of which one in each pair contradicts the other, but each of which necessarily belongs to metaphysics, by which it must either be accepted or rejected (although there is not one that has not in its time been accepted by some philosopher). Now he has the liberty of selecting any one of these eight propositions at his pleasure and accepting it without any proof, of which I shall make him a present, but only one (for waste of time will be just as little serviceable to him as to me), and then of attacking my proof of the opposite proposition. If I can save this one and at the same time show that, according to principles which every dogmatic metaphysics must necessarily recognize, the contrary of the proposition adopted by him can be just as clearly proved, it is thereby established that metaphysics has an hereditary failing not to be explained, much less set aside, until we ascend to its birthplace, pure reason itself. And thus my *Critique* must either be accepted or a better one take its place; at least it must be studied, which is the only thing I now require. If, on the other hand, I cannot save my demonstration, then a synthetic proposition *a priori* from dogmatic principles is to be reckoned to the score of my opponent, and I shall deem my impeachment of ordinary metaphysics unjust and pledge myself to

51. [The theses and antitheses of "The Antinomy of Pure Reason" in the *Critique*, B 454–489]

recognize his censure of my *Critique* as justified (although this would not be the consequence by a long way). To this end it would be necessary, it seems to me, that he should step out of his incognito. Otherwise I do not see how it could be avoided that, instead of dealing with one, I should be honored or besieged by several challenges coming from anonymous and 380 unqualified opponents.

Proposals as to an Investigation of the
Critique *upon which a Judgement May Follow*

I feel obliged to the learned public even for the silence with which it for a long time honored my *Critique,* for this proves at least a postponement of judgment and some supposition that, in a work leaving all beaten tracks and striking out on a new path, in which one cannot at once perhaps so easily find one's way, something may perchance lie from which an important but at present dead branch of human knowledge may derive new life and productiveness. Hence may have originated a solicitude for the as yet tender shoot, lest it be destroyed by a hasty judgment. A specimen of a judgment, delayed for the above reasons, is now before my eye in the *Gothaische gelehrte Zeitung,* [52] the thoroughness of which (leaving out of account my praise, which might be suspicious) every reader will himself perceive from the clear and unperverted presentation of a fragment of one of the first principles of my work.

Since an extensive structure cannot be judged at once as a whole from a hurried glance, I propose that it be tested piece by piece from its foundation up, and in this, the present *Prolegomena* may be used as a general outline with which the work itself may conveniently be compared. This suggestion, if it were founded on nothing more than my conceit of importance, such as vanity ordinarily attributes to all of one's own productions, would be immodest and would deserve to be rejected with indig-

52. [The issue of August 24, 1782]

nation. But now the interests of all speculative philosophy have arrived at the point of total extinction, while human reason hangs upon them with inextinguishable affection; and only after having been endlessly disappointed, does it vainly attempt to change this into indifference.

In our thinking age, it is not to be supposed but that many deserving men would use any good opportunity of working for the common interest of an ever more enlightened reason, if there were only some hope of attaining the goal. Mathematics, natural science, laws, arts, even morality, etc. do not completely fill the soul; there is always a space left over reserved for pure and speculative reason, the emptiness of which prompts us to seek in vagaries, buffooneries, and mysticism for what seems to be employment and entertainment, but what actually is mere pastime undertaken in order to deaden the troublesome voice of reason, which, in accordance with its nature, requires something that can satisfy it and does not merely subserve other ends or the interests of our inclinations. A consideration, therefore, which is concerned only with this extent of reason as it subsists for itself has, as I may reasonably suppose, a great fascination for everyone who has attempted thus to extend his concept, and I may even say a greater fascination than any other theoretical branch of knowledge, for which he would not willingly exchange it because here all other branches of knowledge and even purposes must meet and unite themselves in a whole.

I offer, therefore, these *Prolegomena* as a plan and guide for this investigation, and not the work itself. Although I am even now perfectly satisfied with the latter as far as contents, order, and mode of presentation, and the care that I have expended in weighing and testing every sentence before writing it down are concerned (for it has taken me years to satisfy myself fully, not only as regards the whole, but in some cases even as to the sources of one particular proposition); yet I am not quite satisfied with my exposition in some sections of the Doctrine of Elements,[53] as for instance in the deduction of the concepts of the understanding or in the chapter on the paralogisms of pure

381

---

53. [The first part of the *Critique of Pure Reason*, the second part being the Methodology]

reason,[54] because a certain diffuseness takes away from their clearness, and in place of them what is here said in the *Prolegomena* respecting these sections may be made the basis of the test.

It is the boast of the Germans that, where steady and continuous industry are requisite, they can carry things further than other nations. If this opinion be well founded, an opportunity, a task, presents itself; the successful issue of this task can scarcely be doubted and all thinking men can equally take part in it, though they have hitherto been unsuccessful in accomplishing it and in thus confirming the above good opinion. This is chiefly because the science in question is of such a special kind that it can all at once be brought to completion and to that permanent   382 state beyond which it can never be developed, in the least degree enlarged by later discoveries, or changed if we leave out of account adornment by greater clearness in some places or additional utility for all sorts of purposes. This is an advantage no other science has or can have, because there is none so completely isolated and independent of others and so exclusively concerned with the faculty of cognition pure and simple. And the present moment seems not to be unfavorable to my expectation; for in Germany no one seems now to know how to occupy himself, apart from the so-called useful sciences, so as to pursue not mere play but a business possessing an enduring purpose.

To discover how the endeavors of the learned may be united in such a purpose I must leave to others. In the meantime, it is not my intention to persuade anyone merely to follow my theses or even to flatter me with the hope that he will do so; but attacks, repetitions, limitations, or confirmation, completion, and extension, as the case may be, should be appended. If the matter be but investigated from its foundation, it cannot fail that a system, albeit not my own, shall be erected that shall be a possession for future generations for which they may have reason to be grateful.

It would lead us too far here to show what kind of metaphysics may be expected when the principles of criticism have been per-

---

54. [These sections were almost entirely rewritten in the second edition of the *Critique* (1787).]

fected and how, though the old false feathers have been pulled out, it need by no means appear poor and reduced to an insignificant figure but may be in other respects richly and respectably adorned. But other and great uses which would result from such a reform strike one immediately. The ordinary metaphysics had its uses, in that it sought out the elementary concepts of the pure understanding in order to make them clear through analysis and determinate through explications. In this way it was a training for reason, in whatever direction it might be turned. But this was all the good it did. This merit was subsequently destroyed when it favored conceit by venturesome assertions, sophistry by subtle dodges and prettifying, and shallowness by the ease with which it decided the most difficult problems by means of a little

383 school wisdom, which is only the more seductive the more it has the choice, on the one hand, of taking on something of the language of science and, on the other, from that of popular discourse—thus being everything to everybody but in reality being nothing at all. By criticism, however, a standard is given to our judgment whereby knowledge may be with certainty distinguished from pseudo-knowledge and firmly founded, being brought into full operation in metaphysics—a mode of thought extending by degrees its beneficial influence over every other use of reason, at once infusing into it the true philosophical spirit. But the service that metaphysics performs also for theology, by making it independent of the judgment of dogmatic speculation and thereby securing it completely against the attacks of all such opponents, is certainly not to be valued lightly. For ordinary metaphysics, although it promised theology much advantage, could not keep this promise, and by summoning speculative dogmatics to its assistance did nothing but arm enemies against itself. Mysticism, which can prosper in a rationalistic age only when it hides itself behind a system of school metaphysics, under the protection of which it may venture to rave with a semblance of rationality, is driven from theology, its last hiding place, by critical philosophy. Last, but not least, it cannot be otherwise than important to a teacher of metaphysics to be able to say with universal assent that what he expounds is *science*, and that by it actual service will be rendered to the commonweal.

GERMAN-ENGLISH LIST OF TERMS

A

Aesthetik	aesthetic
Akzidenz	accident
Allgemeingültigkeit	universal validity
Allheit	totality
Analogie	analogy
Analogien der Erfahrung	analogies of experience
Analytik	analytic
analytische Methode	analytic method
analytische Sätze	analytic propositions
Anfang	beginning
Anschauung	intuition
Anthropologie	anthropology
Anthropomorphismus	anthropomorphism
Antinomie der reinen Vernunft	antinomy of pure reason
Antizipationen der Wahrnehmung	anticipations of perception
Apperzeption	apperception
Arithmetik	arithmetic
Astronomie	astronomy
Attraktion	attraction
Aufgabe	problem
Axiom	axiom
Axiome der Anschauung	axioms of intuition

B

Bedingung	condition
Begriff	concept
Beharrlichkeit	permanence
Bewegung	motion
Bewußtsein	consciousness

C

Chemie	chemistry

D

Dasein	existence
Deduktion	deduction, justification
Deismus	deism
Denken	thinking
Dialektik	dialectic
Ding an sich	thing in itself
discursiv	discursive
Dogmatik	dogmatics
dogmatisch	dogmatic
Dogmatismus	dogmatism
Dynamik	dynamics
dynamische Grundsätze	dynamic principles

E

Einbildungskraft	imagination
Einfache, das	simple
Einheit	unity
Einschränkung	limitation
Elementarbegriff	elementary concept
Elementarerkenntnis	elementary cognition
Empfindung	sensation
Erfahrung	experience
Erfahrungsurteil	judgment of experience
Erkenntnis	cognition, knowledge

Erläuterungsurteil	explicative judgment	immanent	immanent
Erscheinung	appearance	Induktion	induction
Erweiterungsurteil	ampliative judgment	intellektuel	intellectual
		Intelligenz	intelligence
		intelligible	intelligible
Etwas	something	intensiv	intensive
extensiv	extensive	intuitiv	intuitive

F

Fatalismus	fatalism	**K**	
Form	form	Kategorie	category
Frage	question	Kausalität	causality
Freiheit	freedom	Kegelschnitte	conic sections
		Konstruktion	construction
		Körper	body

G

		Kraft	force
Gefühl	feeling	Kritik	critique, criticism
Gegenstand	object		
gemeiner Menschenverstand	common sense	**L**	
Gemeinschaft	community	Leben	life
Geometrie	geometry	Logik	logic
Gesetz	law	Logiker	logician
Gewohnheit	habit	logisch	logical
Glaube	belief		
Gott	God	**M**	
Grad	degree	Materialismus	materialism
Grammatik	grammar	Materie	matter
Grenze	bounds	Mathematik	mathematics
Größe	quantity	mathematische Grundsätze	mathematical principles
Grundsatz	principle	Mechanik	mechanics
Gültigkeit	validity	Metaphysik	metaphysics
		Metaphysiker	metaphysician

H

		metaphysisch	metaphysical
Handlung	action	Methode	method
höchstes Wesen	Supreme Being	Methodenlehre	doctrine of method
hyperphysisch	hyperphysical	Modalität	modality
Hypothese	hypothesis	Möglichkeit	possibility
		Momente	moments
		Moral	morals

I

		moralisch	moral
Ich, das	ego		
Ideal	ideal	**N**	
Idealismus	idealism	Natur	nature
Idealität	ideality	Naturalismus	naturalism
Idee	idea	Naturgeschichte	history of nature
Identität	identity	Naturgesetz	law of nature

Naturnotwendigkeit	natural necessity	Religion	religion
Naturphilosophie	philosophy of nature	Rhapsodie	rhapsody
Natursystem	system of nature		S
Naturwissenschaft	natural science	Schein	illusion
Negation	negation	Schema	schema
Nichts	nothing	Schematismus	schematism
Notwendigkeit	necessity	Schwärmerei	vagaries
Noumena	noumena	Seele	soul
Null	zero	Sinne	sense
		Sinnenwelt	sensible world
		Sinnlichkeit	sensibility
	O	Skeptizismus	scepticism
Ontologie	ontology	Sollen, das	ought
ontologisch	ontological	Subjekt	subject
		Substanz	substance
		Synthesis	synthesis
	P	synthetisch	synthetic
Paralogismus	paralogism	synthetische Sätze	synthetic propositions
Phänomenologie	phenomenology		
Philosophie	philosophy	System	system
Phoronomie	phoronomy		
Physik	physics		T
physiologisch	physiological	Tafel	table
Postprädikamente	post-predicaments	Teilbarkeit	divisibility
Postulate	postulates	Theismus	theism
Prädikabilien	predicables	Theologie	theology
Prädikamente	predicaments	Tod	death
Prinzip	principle	Trägheit	inertia
Psychologie	psychology	transscendent	transcendent
psychologisch	psychological	transscendental	transcendental
		Transscendental-philosophie	transcendental philosophy
	Q		
Qualität	quality		
Quantität	quantity		U
		Unbegreiflichkeit	incomprehensibility
	R	Undurchdringlichkeit	impenetrability
Raum	space		
Realisten	realists	Unendlichkeit	infinity
Realität	reality	Unmöglichkeit	impossibility
Reflexionsbegriffe	concepts of reflection	Ursache	cause
Regel	rule	Urteil	judgment
Relation	relation	Urteilen, das	judging
		Urwesen	original being

V

Vereinigung	unification
Vernunft	reason
Vernunftbegriffe	concepts of reason
Vernunftgründe	grounds of reason
Verstand	understanding
Verstandesbegriffe	concepts of the understanding
Verstandeswesen	beings of the understanding
Vielheit	plurality
Vollkommenheit	completeness
Vorstellung	representation

W

Wahrheit	truth
Wahrnehmung	perception
Wahrnehmungsurteil	judgment of perception

Wahrscheinlichkeit	probability
Welt	world
Widerspruch	contradiction
Wirklichkeit	actuality
Wirkung und Gegenwirkung	action and reaction
Wissen	knowing
Wissenschaft	science

Z

Zeit	time
Zufall	contingent
zureichender Grund	sufficient reason
Zusammengesetztes	composite
Zusammensetzung	combination
Zweck	purpose

INDEX

(Roman numerals refer to the Translator's Foreword and Introduction; Arabic ones refer to the page numbers of the Akademie edition, which appear as marginal numbers in the present translation.)

Accidents (*Akzidenzen*) of a substance, 308, 333, 368

Action (*Handlung*), 315; spontaneity and freedom, 344–346; of God, 344n; as a derivative concept of causality, 257; *see also* Causality, Freedom

Action and reaction (*Wirkung und Gegenwirkung*), 307; *see also* Community

Actuality (*Wirklichkeit*), as a pure category of the understanding, 308; of a thing (in contrast to logical being), 294

Aesthetic (*Aesthetik*), transcendental, 315, 318

Aggregate (*Aggregat*), 310; *see also* System

Alchemy (*Alchimie*), 366

Ampliative judgments (*Erweiterungsurteile*), 266–270; *see also* Judgment, synthetic

Analogical knowledge of God, *see* As if

Analogies of experience (*Analogien der Erfahrung*), xii, 303, 307–312, 335

Analogy (*Analogie*), allowable in empirical natural science, 369

Analytic (*Analytik*), as a part of logic, 276n, 331; *see also* Dialectic

Analytic method (*analytische Methode*), viii–ix, 263, 275, 276n, 279, 365, 368; *see also* Synthetic method

Analytic propositions (*analytische Sätze*), xiv, 266–267, 269, 270, 294, 305, 319

Anthropology (*Anthropologie*), 362

Anthropomorphism (*Anthropomorphismus*), 356, 358–359; dogmatic and symbolic, 357; objective, 358

Anticipations of perception (*Antizipationen der Wahrnehmung*), 303, 306–307

Antinomy of pure reason (*Antinomie der reinen Vernunft*), 292, 330, 333, 379; the mathematical ones, 341, 343; the first one, 341–342; the second one, 342; the dynamical ones, 343; the third one, 343–347; the fourth one, 347

A posteriori, 267, 275, 281, 294, 305n

Appearance (*Erscheinung*), as representation of our sensuous intuition, 287–288, 314–315; as empirical representation, 283–284, 290–293, 307, 319, 342; as the matter of experience, 309; in contrast to the internal constitution of things, xi, 352–353, 361, 374–375; as internal phenomena of our soul, 334; internal and external appearances, 336–337; in contrast to illusion, 314–316, 339–341, 343; *see* Thing in itself (the contrary of Appearance)

Apperception (*Apperzeption*), ix, 318, 334n

A priori, 267, 270, 275, 277–278, 279, 280, 281, 319, 373n, 375

127